CAMBRIDGE LIBRARY COLLECTION

Books of enduring scholarly value

History

The books reissued in this series include accounts of historical events and movements by eye-witnesses and contemporaries, as well as landmark studies that assembled significant source materials or developed new historiographical methods. The series includes work in social, political and military history on a wide range of periods and regions, giving modern scholars ready access to influential publications of the past.

Secret History

Leonora Mary Hassal Sansay (b. 1781), also known as Mary Hassal, was U.S. Vice-President Aaron Burr's niece. This work, first published in 1808, takes the form of a series of letters to her uncle, describing the events which she witnessed between 1802 and 1805 in the French colony of St Domingo, which became the Republic of Haiti in 1804 after a fierce revolution. A large French army under General Leclerc was sent by Napoleon to retake the colony from the ex-slave Toussaint Louverture and his army. Hassal depicts life under the French occupation, and also in Cuba and Jamaica, to which many settlers from St Domingo fled. She comments particularly on the position and occupations of women, but regrets their subjection to and dependence on men. The tone is anecdotal, but the volume will be of interest to social historians as an eyewitness account of a turbulent period.

Cambridge University Press has long been a pioneer in the reissuing of out-of-print titles from its own backlist, producing digital reprints of books that are still sought after by scholars and students but could not be reprinted economically using traditional technology. The Cambridge Library Collection extends this activity to a wider range of books which are still of importance to researchers and professionals, either for the source material they contain, or as landmarks in the history of their academic discipline.

Drawing from the world-renowned collections in the Cambridge University Library, and guided by the advice of experts in each subject area, Cambridge University Press is using state-of-the-art scanning machines in its own Printing House to capture the content of each book selected for inclusion. The files are processed to give a consistently clear, crisp image, and the books finished to the high quality standard for which the Press is recognised around the world. The latest print-on-demand technology ensures that the books will remain available indefinitely, and that orders for single or multiple copies can quickly be supplied.

The Cambridge Library Collection will bring back to life books of enduring scholarly value (including out-of-copyright works originally issued by other publishers) across a wide range of disciplines in the humanities and social sciences and in science and technology.

Secret History

Or, The Horrors of St. Domingo,
in a Series of Letters

MARY HASSAL

CAMBRIDGE UNIVERSITY PRESS

Cambridge, New York, Melbourne, Madrid, Cape Town, Singapore,
São Paolo, Delhi, Dubai, Tokyo, Mexico City

Published in the United States of America by Cambridge University Press, New York

www.cambridge.org
Information on this title: www.cambridge.org/9781108024433

© in this compilation Cambridge University Press 2010

This edition first published 1808
This digitally printed version 2010

ISBN 978-1-108-02443-3 Paperback

SECRET HISTORY;

OR,

THE HORRORS OF ST. DOMINGO,

IN

A SERIES OF LETTERS,

WRITTEN BY A LADY AT CAPE FRANCOIS,

TO

COLONEL BURR,

LATE VICE-PRESIDENT OF THE UNITED STATES,

PRINCIPALLY DURING THE COMMAND OF

GENERAL ROCHAMBEAU.

PHILADELPHIA:

PUBLISHED BY BRADFORD & INSKEEP.

R. CARR, PRINTER.

•••••••••••

1808.

PREFACE.

I AM fearful of having been led into an error by my friends, when taught by them to believe that I could write something which would interest and please; and it was chiefly with a view to ascertain what confidence I might place in their kind assurances on this subject, that I collected and consented, though reluctantly, to the publication of these letters.

Should a less partial public give them a favourable reception, and allow them to possess some merit, it would encourage me to endeavour to obtain their further approbation by a little work already planned and in some forwardness.

THE AUTHOR.

Philadelphia, Nov. 30th, 1807.

LETTER I.

Cape Francois.

WE arrived safely here, my dear friend, after a passage of forty days, during which I suffered horribly from sea-sickness, heat and confinement; but the society of my fellow-passengers was so agreeable that I often forgot the inconvenience to which I was exposed. It consisted of five or six French families who, having left St. Domingo at the beginning of the revolution, were now returning full of joy at the idea of again possessing the estates from which they had been driven by their revolted slaves. Buoyed by their newly awakened hopes they were all delightful anticipation. There is an elasticity in the French character which repels misfortune. They have an inexhaustible flow of spirits that bears them lightly through the ills of life.

B

Towards the end of the voyage, when I was well enough to go on deck, I was delighted with the profound tranquillity of the ocean, the uninterrupted view, the beautiful horizon, and wished, since fate has separated me from those I love, that I could build a dwelling on the bosom of the waters, where, sheltered from the storms that agitate mankind, I should be exposed to those of heaven only. But a truce to melancholy reflections, for here I am in St. Domingo, with a new world opening to my view.

My sister, whose fortunes, you know, I was obliged to follow, repents every day having so precipitately chosen a husband: it is impossible for two creatures to be more different, and I foresee that she will be wretched.

On landing, we found the town a heap of ruins. A more terrible picture of desolation cannot be imagined. Passing through streets choaked with rubbish, we reached with difficulty a house which had escaped the general fate. The people live in tents, or make a kind of shelter, by laying a few boards across the half-consumed beams; for the buildings being

here of hewn stone, with walls three feet thick,
only the roofs and floors have been destroyed.
But to hear of the distress which these unfortunate people have suffered, would fill with
horror the stoutest heart, and make the most
obdurate melt with pity.

When the French fleet appeared before
the mouth of the harbour, Christophe, the
Black general, who commanded at the Cape,
rode through the town, ordering all the women
to leave their houses—the men had been taken
to the plain the day before, for he was going
to set fire to the place, which he did with his
own hand.

The ladies, bearing their children in their
arms, or supporting the trembling steps of
their aged mothers, ascended in crowds the
mountain which rises behind the town. Climb-
ing over rocks covered with brambles, where
no path had been ever beat, their feet were torn
to pieces and their steps marked with blood.
Here they suffered all the pains of hunger and
thirst; the most terrible apprehensions for their
fathers, husbands, brothers and sons; to which
was added the sight of the town in flames: and

even these horrors were increased by the ex-
plosion of the powder magazine. Large masses of rock were detached by the shock, which,
rolling down the sides of the mountain, many
of these hapless fugitives were killed. Others
still more unfortunate, had their limbs broken
or sadly bruised, whilst their wretched companions could offer them nothing but unavail-
ing sympathy and impotent regret.

On the third day the negroes evacuated
the place, and the fleet entered the harbour.
Two gentlemen, who had been concealed by
a faithful slave, went in a canoe to meet the
admiral's vessel, and arrived in time to prevent a dreadful catastrophe.   The general,
seeing numbers of people descending the
mountain, thought they were the negroes coming to oppose his landing and was preparing
to fire on them, when these gentlemen informed him that they were the white inhabitants,
and thus prevented a mistake too shocking to
be thought of.

The men now entered from the plain and
sought among the smoking ruins the objects
of their affectionate solicitude. To paint these

heart-rending scenes of tenderness and woe, description has no powers. The imagination itself shrinks from the task.

Three months after this period we arrived and have now been a month here, the town is rapidly rebuilding, but it is extremely difficult to find a lodging. The heat is intolerable and the season so unhealthy that the people die in incredible numbers. On the night of our arrival, Toussaint the general in chief of the negroes, was seized at the Gonaives and embarked for France. This event caused great rejoicing. A short time before he was taken, he had his treasure buried in the woods, and at the return of the negroes he employed on this expedition, they were shot without being suffered to utter a word.

Clara has had the yellow fever. Her husband, who certainly loves her very much, watched her with unceasing care, and I believe, preserved her life, to which however she attaches no value since it must be passed with him.

Nothing amuses her. She sighs continually for the friend of her youth and seems to exist only in the recollection of past happiness. Her aversion to her husband is unqualified and unconquerable. He is vain, illiterate, talkative. A silent fool may be borne, but from a loquacious one there is no relief. How painful must her intercourse with him be; and how infinitely must that pain be augmented by the idea of being his forever? Her elegant mind, stored with literary acquirements, is lost to him. Her proud soul is afflicted at depending on one she abhors, and at beholding her form, and you know that form so vilely bartered. Whilst on the continent she was less sensible of the horrors of her fate. The society of her friend gave a charm to her life, and having married in compliance with his advice, she thought that she would eventually be happy. But their separation has rent the veil which concealed her heart; she finds no sympathy in the bosom of her husband. She is alone and she is wretched.

General Le Clerc is small, his face is interesting, but he has an appearance of ill health. His wife, the sister of Buonaparte, lives in a house on the mountain till there can be one in town prepared for her reception. She is offended, and I think justly, with the ladies of the Cape, who, from a mistaken pride, did not wait on her when she arrived, because having lost their cloaths they could not dazzle her with their finery.

Having heard that there were some American ladies here she expressed a desire to see them; Mr. V— proposed to present us; Clara, who would not walk a mile to see a queen, declined. But I, who walk at all times, merely for the pleasure it affords me, went; and, considering the labour it costs to ascend the mountain, I have a claim on the gratitude of Madame for having undertaken it to shew her an object which she probably expected to find in a savage state.

She was in a room darkened by Venetian blinds, lying on her sofa, from which she half rose to receive me. When I was seated she reclined again on the sofa and amused general Boyer, who sat at her feet, by letting her slipper fall continually, which he respectfully put on as often as it fell. She is small, fair, with blue eyes and flaxen hair. Her face is expres-

sive of sweetness but without spirit. She has
a voluptuous mouth, and is rendered interesting by an air of languor which spreads itself
over her whole frame. She was dressed in a
muslin morning gown, with a Madras handkerchief on her head. I gave her one of the
beautiful silver medals of Washington, en-
graved by Reich, with which she seemed
much pleased. The conversation languished,
and I soon withdrew.

General Le Clerc had gone in the morning
to fort Dauphin.

I am always in good spirits, for every thing
here charms me by its novelty. There are a
thousand pretty things to be had, new fashions
and elegant trinkets from Paris; but we have
no balls, no plays, and of what use is finery if
it cannot be shewn?

The natives of this country murmur already against the general in chief; they say he
places too much confidence in the negroes.
When Toussaint was seized he had all the
black chiefs in his power, and, by embarking
them for France, he would have spread terror
throughout the Island, and the negroes would

have been easily reduced, instead of which he relies on their good faith, has them continually in his house, at his table, and wastes the time in conference which should be differently employed. The Creoles shake their heads and predict much ill. Accustomed to the climate, and acquainted with the manner of fighting the Negroes, they offer advice, which is not listened to; nor are any of them employed, but all places of honour or emolument are held by Europeans, who appear to regard the Island as a place to be conquered and divided among the victors, and are consequently viewed by the natives with a jealous eye. Indeed the professed intention of those who have come with the army, is to make a fortune, and return to France with all possible speed, to enjoy it. It cannot be imagined that they will be very delicate about the means of accomplishing their purpose.

The Cape is surrounded; at least the plain is held by the Negroes; but the town is tranquil, and Dessalines and the other black chiefs are on the best terms with general Le Clerc.

We are to have a grand review next week.

The militia is to be organized, and the general is to address the troops on the field.   He
has the reputation of being very eloquent, but
he has shocked every body by having ordered
a superb service of plate, made of the money
intended to pay the army, while the poor soldiers, badly cloathed, and still more badly fed,
are asking alms in the street, and absolutely
dying of want.

A beggar had never been known in this
country, and to see them in such numbers,
fills the inhabitants with horror; but why
should such trifling considerations as the preservation of soldiers, prevent a general in chief
from eating out of silver dishes?

We have neither public nor private balls,
nor any amusement except now and then a
little scandal.   The most current at this moment is, that Madame Le Clerc is very kind
to general Boyer, and that her husband is not
content, which in a French husband is a little
extraordinary.   Perhaps the last part of the
anecdote is calumny.

Madame Le Clerc, as I learned from a
gentleman who has long known her, betrayed

from her earliest youth a disposition to gallantry, and had, when very young, some adventures of eclat in Marseilles. Her brother,
whose favourite she is, married her to general
Le Clerc, to whom he gave the command of
the army intended to sail for St. Domingo,
after having given that island, as a marriage
portion, to his sister. But her reluctance to
come to this country was so great, that it was
almost necessary to use force to oblige her to
embark.

She has one child, a lovely boy, three years
old, of which she appears very fond. But for
a young and beautiful woman, accustomed to
the sweets of adulation, and the intoxicating
delights of Paris, certainly the transition to this
country, in its present state, has been too violent. She has no society, no amusement, and
never having imagined that she would be
forced to seek an equivalent for either in the
resources of her own mind, she has made no
provision for such an unforeseen emergency.

She hates reading, and though passionately fond of music plays on no instrument; never having stolen time from her pleasurable

pursuits to devote to the acquisition of that
divine art. She can do nothing but dance,
and to dance alone is a triste resource; therefore it cannot be surprising if her early pro-
pensities predominate, and she listens to the
tale of love breathed by General Boyer, for
never did a more fascinating votary offer his
vows at the Idalian shrine. His form and face
are models of masculine perfection; his eyes
sparkle with enthusiasm, and his voice is mo-
dulated by a sweetness of expression which
cannot be heard without emotion. Thus situated, and thus surrounded, her youth and
beauty plead for her, and those most disposed
to condemn would exclaim on beholding her:

" If to her share some female errors fall,
Look in her face, and you'll forget them all."

I suppose you'll laugh at this gossip, but
'tis the news of the day, nothing is talked of
but Madame Le Clerc, and envy and ill-na-
ture pursue her because she is charming and
surrounded by splendor.

I have just now been reading Madame De
Stael on the passions, which she describes

very well, but I believe not precisely as she
felt their influence. I have heard an anecdote
of her which I admire ; a friend, to whom she
had communicated her intention of publishing
her memoirs, asked what she intended doing
with the gallant part,—Oh, she replied, je ne
me peindrai qu'en buste.

LETTER II.

Cape Francois.

What a change has taken place here since my last letter was written ! I mentioned that there was to be a grand review, and I also mentioned that the confidence General Le Clerc placed in the negroes was highly blamed, and justly, as he has found to his cost. On the day of the review, when the troops of the line and the guarde nationale were assembled on the field, a plot was discovered, which had been formed by the negroes in the town, to seize the arsenal and to point the cannon of a fort, which overlooked the place of review, on the troops ; whilst Clairvaux, the mulatto general, who commanded the advanced posts, was to join the negroes of the plain, overpower the guards, and entering the town, complete the destruction of the white inhabi-

tants. The first part of the plot was discovered and defeated. But Clairvaux made good
his escape, and in the evening attacked the
post General Le Clerc had so imprudently
confided to him. The consternation was
terrible. The guarde nationale, composed
chiefly of Creoles, did wonders. The American captains and sailors volunteered their
services ; they fought bravely, and many of
them perished. The negroes were repulsed;
but if they gained no ground they lost none,
and they occupy at present the same posts as
before. The pusillanimous General Le Clerc,
shrinking from danger of which his own im-
prudence had been the cause, thought only of
saving himself. He sent his plate and valuable effects on board the admiral's vessel, and
was preparing to embark secretly with his
suite, but the brave admiral La Touche de
Treville sent him word that he would fire with
more pleasure on those who abandoned the
town, than on those who attacked it.

The ensuing morning presented a dreadful spectacle. Nothing was heard but the
groans of the wounded, who were carried

through the streets to their homes, and the cries of the women for their friends who were slain.

The general, shut up in his house, would see nobody; ashamed of the weakness which had led to this disastrous event, and of the want of courage he had betrayed : a fever seized him and he died in three days.

Madame Le Clerc, who had not loved him whilst living, mourned his death like the Ephesian matron, cut off her hair, which was very beautiful, to put it in his coffin; refused all sustenance and all public consolation.

General Rochambeau, who is at Port au Prince, has been sent for by the inhabitants of the Cape to take the command. Much good is expected from the change, he is said to be a brave officer and an excellent man.

Monsieur D'Or is in the interim Captain General, and unites in himself the three principal places in the government : Prefect Colonial, Ordonnateur, and General in Chief.

All this bustle would be delightful if it was not attended with such melancholy consequences. It keeps us from petrifying, of which I was in danger.

I have become acquainted with some Creole ladies who, having staid in the Island during the revolution, relate their sufferings in a
manner which harrows up the soul; and dwell
on the recollection of their long lost happiness
with melancholy delight. St. Domingo was
formerly a garden. Every inhabitant lived on
his estate like a Sovereign ruling his slaves
with despotic sway, enjoying all that luxury
could invent, or fortune procure.

The pleasures of the table were carried to
the last degree of refinement. Gaming knew
no bounds, and libertinism, called love, was
without restraint. The Creole is generous
hospitable, magnificent, but vain, inconstant,
and incapable of serious application ; and in
this abode of pleasure and luxurious ease vices
have reigned at which humanity must shudder.
The jealousy of the women was often terrible
in its consequences. One lady, who had a
beautiful negro girl continually about her person, thought she saw some symptoms of *ten-
dresse* in the eyes of her husband, and all the
furies of jealousy seized her soul.

She ordered one of her slaves to cut off the

head of the unfortunate victim, which was instantly done. At dinner her husband said he felt no disposition to eat, to which his wife, with the air of a demon, replied, perhaps I can give you something that will excite your appetite; it has at least had that effect before. She rose and drew from a closet the head of Coomba. The husband, shocked beyond expression, left the house and sailed immediately for France, in order never again to behold such a monster.

Many similar anecdotes have been related by my Creole friends; but one of them, after having excited my warmest sympathy, made me laugh heartily in the midst of my tears: She told me that her husband was stabbed in her arms by a slave whom he had always treated as his brother; that she had seen her children killed, and her house burned, but had been herself preserved by a faithful slave, and conducted, after incredible sufferings, and through innumerable dangers to the Cape. The same slave, she added, and the idea seemed to console her for every other loss, saved all my madrass handkerchiefs.

The Creole ladies have an air of voluptuous languor which renders them extremely
interesting. Their eyes, their teeth, and their
hair are remarkably beautiful, and they have
acquired from the habit of commanding their
slaves, an air of dignity which adds to their
charms. Almost too indolent to pronounce
their words they speak with a drawling accent
that is very agreeable : but since they have
been roused by the pressure of misfortune
many of them have displayed talents and found
resources in the energy of their own minds
which it would have been supposed impossible
for them to possess.

They have naturally a taste for music;
dance with a lightness, a grace, an elegance
peculiar to themselves, and those who, having been educated in France, unite the French
vivacity to the Creole sweetness, are the most
irresistible creatures that the imagination can
conceive. In the ordinary intercourse of life
they are delightful; but if I wanted a friend on
any extraordinary occasion I would not venture to rely on their stability.

LETTER III.

—

Cape Francois.

The so much desired general Rochambeau
is at length here.　His arrival was announced,
not by the ringing of bells, for they have none,
but by the firing of cannon.　Every body, except myself went to see him land, and I was
prevented, not by want of curiosity, but by in-
disposition.　Nothing is heard of but the public joy.　He is considered as the guardian, as
the saviour of the people.　Every proprietor
feels himself already on his habitation and I
have even heard some of them disputing about
the quality of the coffee they expect soon to
gather; perhaps these sanguine Creoles may
find that they have reckoned without their host.

However, *en attendant*, the General, who
it seems bears pleasure as well as conquest in

his train, gives a grand ball on Thursday next. We are invited, and we go.

Clara is delighted! for the first time since our arrival her eyes brightened at receiving the invitation, and the important subject of what colours are to be worn, what fashions adopted, is continually discussed. Her husband, whose chief pleasure is to see her brilliant, indulges all the extravagance of her capricious taste. She sighs for conquest because she is a stranger to content, and will enter into every scheme of dissipation with eagerness to forget for a moment her internal wretchedness. She is unhappy, though surrounded by splendor, because from the constitution of her mind she cannot derive happiness from an object that does not interest her heart.

My letter shall not be closed till after the ball of which I suppose you will be glad to have a description.

But why do you not write to me?

I am ignorant of your pursuits and even of the place of your abode, and though convinced that you cannot forget me, I am afflicted if I do not receive assurances of your friendship by every vessel that arrives !

Clara has not written, for nothing has hitherto had power to rouse her from the lethargy into which she had sunk. Perhaps the scenes of gaiety in which she is now going to engage may dispell the gloom which threatened to destroy all the energy of her charming mind. Perhaps too these scenes may be more fatal to her peace than the gloom of which I complain, for in this miserable world we know not what to desire. The accomplishment of our wishes is often a real misfortune. We pass our lives in searching after happiness, and how many die without having found it !

In Continuation.

Well my dear friend the ball is over—that ball of which I promised you a description. But who can describe the heat or suffocating sensations felt in a crowd ?

The General has an agreeable face, a sweet mouth, and most enchanting smile ; but

" Like the sun, he shone on all alike,"

and paid no particular attention to any object. His uniform was *a la hussar*, and very brilliant; he wore red boots:—but his person is bad, he is too short ; a Bacchus-like figure, which accords neither with my idea of a great General nor a great man.

But you know one of my faults is to create objects in my imagination on the model of my incomparable friend, and then to dislike every thing I meet because it falls short of my expectations.

I was disappointed at the ball, because I was confounded in the crowd, but my disappointment was trifling compared with that felt by Clara. Accustomed to admiration she expected to receive it on this occasion in no moderate portion, and to find herself undistinguished was not flattering. She did not dance, staid only an hour, and has declared against all balls in future. But there is one announced by the Admiral which may perhaps induce her to change her resolution.

Madame Le Clerc has sailed for France with the body of her husband, which was embalmed here.

The place is tranquil.   The arrival of General Rochambeau seems to have spread terror
among the negroes.   I wish they were reduced
to order that I might see the so much vaunted
habitations where I should repose beneath the
shade of orange groves ; walk on carpets of
rose leaves and frenchipone; be fanned to sleep
by silent slaves, or have my feet tickled into
extacy by the soft hand of a female attendant.

Such were the pleasures of the Creole ladies
whose time was divided between the bath, the
table, the toilette and the lover.

What a delightful existence ! thus to pass
away life in the arms of voluptuous indolence;
to wander over flowery fields of unfading ver-
dure, or through forests of majestic palm-trees,
sit by a fountain bursting from a savage rock
frequented only by the cooing dove, and indulge in these enchanting solitudes all the re-
veries of an exalted imagination.

But the moment of enjoying these pleasures is, I fear, far distant.   The negroes have
felt during ten years the blessing of liberty,
for a blessing it certainly is, however acquired,
and they will not be easily deprived of it.   they

have fought and vanquished the French troops, and their strengh has increased from a know-ledge of the weakness of their opposers, and the climate itself combats for them. Inured to a savage life they lay in the woods without being injured by the sun, the dew or the rain. A negro eats a plantain, a sour orange, the herbs and roots of the field, and requires no cloathing, whilst this mode of living is fatal to the European soldiers. The sun and the dew are equally fatal to them, and they have perished in such numbers that, if reinforcements do not arrive, it will soon be impossible to defend the town.

The country is entirely in the hands of the negroes, and whilst their camp abounds in provisions, every thing in town is extremely scarce and enormously dear.

Every evening several old Creoles, who live near us, assemble at our house, and talk of their affairs. One of them, whose annual income before the revolution was fifty thou-sand dollars, which he always exceeded in his expenses, now lives in a miserable hut and prolongs with the greatest difficulty his wretch-

ed existence. Yet he still hopes for better
days, in which hope they all join him. The
distress they feel has not deprived them of
their gaiety. They laugh, they sing, they join
in the dance with the young girls of the neighbourhood, and seem to forget their cares in the
prospect of having them speedily removed.

LETTER IV.

—

Cape Francois.

The ball announced by the admiral exceeded all expectations and we are still all extacy. Boats, covered with carpets, conveyed
the company from the shore to the vessel,
which was anchored about half a mile from
the land, and on entering the ball room a fairy
palace presented itself to the view. The decks
were floored in; a roof of canvas was suspended over the whole length of the vessel, which
reached the floor on each side, and formed a
beautiful apartment. Innumerable lustres of
chrystal and wreaths of natural flowers ornamented the cieling; and rose and orange-trees,
in full blossom, ranged round the room, filled
the air with fragrance. The seats were ele-
vated, and separated from the part appropri-
ated to dancing, by a light balustrade. A gal-

lery for the musicians was placed round the
main-mast, and the whole presented to the eye
an elegant saloon, raised by magic in a wil-
derness of sweets. Clara and myself, accompanied by her husband and Major B——,
were among the first who arrived. Never had
I beheld her so interesting. A robe of white
crape shewed to advantage the contours of her
elegant person. Her arms and bosom were
bare; her black hair, fastened on the top with
a brilliant comb, was ornamented by a rose
which seemed to have been thrown there by
accident.

We were presented to the admiral, who
appeared struck by the figure of Clara, and
was saying some very flattering things, when
a flourish of martial music announced the arrival of the General in chief. The admiral
hastened to meet him, and they walked round
the room together.

When the dances began the general leaned
against the orchestra opposite Clara. Her eyes
met his. She bent them to the ground, raised
them timidly and found those of the general
fixed on her: a glow of crimson suffused itself

over her face and bosom. I observed her at-
tentively and knew it was the flush of triumph!
She declined dancing, but when the walses
began she was led out. Those who have not
seen Clara walse know not half her charms.
There is a physiognomy in her form! every
motion is full of soul. The gracefulness of
her arms is unequalled, and she is lighter than
gossamer.

The eyes of the general dwelt on her alone,
and I heard him inquire of several who she
was.

The walse finished, she walked round the
room leaning on the arm of Major B——.
The general followed, and meeting her husband, asked (pointing to Clara) if he knew the
name of that lady. Madame St. Louis, was
the reply. I thought she was an American said
the general. So she is, replied St Louis, but
her husband is a Frenchman. That's true, added the general, but they say he is a d——d
jealous fool, is he here? He has the honour of
answering you, said St Louis. The general
was embarrassed for a moment, but recover-
ing himself said, I am not surprised at your

being jealous, for she is a charming creature.
And he continued uttering so many flattering
things that St. Louis was in the best humour
imaginable. When Clara heard the story,
she laughed, and, I saw, was delighted with
a conquest she now considered assured.

When she sat down, Major B—— presented the General to her, and his pointed attention rendered her the object of universal
admiration. He retired at midnight : the ball
continued. An elegant collation was served
up, and at sunrise we returned home !

The admiral is a very agreeable man, and
I would prefer him, as a lover, to any of his
officers, though he is sixty years old. His
manners are affable and perfectly elegant; his
figure graceful and dignified, and his conversation sprightly. He joined the dance at the
request of a lady, with all the spirit of youth,
and appeared to enjoy the pleasure which his
charming fête diffused.

He told Clara that he would twine a wreath
of myrtle to crown her, for she had vanquished the General. She replied, that she would
mingle it with laurel, and lay it at his feet for

having, by preserving the Cape, given her an opportunity of making the conquest.

Nothing is heard of but balls and parties. Monsieur D'Or gives a concert every Thursday; the General in chief every Sunday : so that from having had no amusement we are in danger of falling into the other extreme, and of being satiated with pleasure.

The Negroes remain pretty tranquil in this quarter; but at Port-au-Prince, and in its neighbourhood, they have been very troublesome.

Jeremie, Les Cayes, and all that part of the island which had been preserved, during the revolution, by the exertions of the inhabitants, have been lost since the appearance of the French troops !

The Creoles complain, and they have cause; for they find in the army sent to defend them, oppressors who appear to seek their destruction. Their houses and their negroes are put under requisition, and they are daily exposed to new vexations.

Some of the ancient inhabitants of the island, who had emigrated, begin to think that their hopes were too sanguine, and that they have returned too soon from the peaceful retreats they found on the continent. They had supposed that the appearance of an army of thirty thousand men would have reduced the negroes to order; but these conquerors of Italy, unnerved by the climate, or from some other cause, lose all their energy, and fly before the undisciplined slaves.

Many of the Creoles, who had remained on the island during the reign of Toussaint, regret the change, and say that they were less vexed by the negroes than by those who have come to protect them.

And these negroes, notwithstanding the state of brutal subjection in which they were kept, have at length acquired a knowledge of their own strength. More than five hundred thousand broke the yoke imposed on them by a few thousand men of a different colour, and claimed the rights of which they had been so cruelly deprived. Unfortunate were those who witnessed the horrible catastrophe which accompanied the first wild transports of freedom! Dearly have they paid for the luxuri-

ous ease in which they revelled at the expense
of these oppressed creatures. Yet even among
these slaves, self-emancipated, and rendered
furious by a desire of vengeance, examples of
fidelity and attachment to their masters have
been found, which do honour to human nature.

For my part, I am all anxiety to return to
the continent. Accustomed from my earliest
infancy to wander on the delightful banks of
the Schuylkill, to meet the keen air on Ken-
sington bridge, and to ramble over the fields
which surround Philadelphia, I feel like a
prisoner in this little place, built on a narrow
strip of land between the sea and a mountain
that rises perpendicularly behind the town.
There is to be sure an opening on one side to
the plain, but the negroes are there encamped; they keep the ground of which general
Le Clerc suffered them to take possession,
and threaten daily to attack the town !

There is no scarcity of beaux here, but
the gallantry of the French officers is fatiguing
from its sameness. They think their appearance alone sufficient to secure a conquest, and

do not conceive it necessary to give their yielding mistresses a decent excuse by paying them a little attention. In three days a love-affair is begun and finished and forgotten ; the first is for the declaration, the second is the day of triumph if it is deferred so long, and the third is for the adieu.

The Creoles do not relish the attacks made on their wives by the officers. The husband of Clara in particular is as jealous as a Turk, and has more than once shewn his displeasure at the pointed attentions of the General-in-chief to his wife, which she encourages, out of contradiction to her husband rather than from any pleasure they afford her. The boisterous gaiety and soldier-like manners of general Rochambeau, can have made no impression on a heart tender and delicate as is that of Clara. But there is a vein of coquetry in her composition which, if indulged, will eventually destroy her peace.

A tragical event happened lately at Port-au-Prince. At a public breakfast, given by the commandant, an officer just arrived from France, addressing himself to a lady, called her *citoyenne.*—The lady observed that she would never answer to that title. The stranger replied that she ought to be proud of being so called. On which her husband, interfering, said that his wife should never answer to any mode of address that she found displeasing. No more passed at that time, but before noon Monsieur C—— received a challenge: the choice of weapons being left to him, he said that it was absolutely indifferent: the stranger insisted on fighting with a rifle; Monsieur C—— replied that he should have no objection to fight with a cannon: it was however, finally settled, that the affair should be decided with pistols; and at sun-rise next morning they met: the officer fired without effect. Monsieur C——, with surer aim laid his antagonist lifeless on the ground.

On what trifles depends the destiny of man! but the Europeans are so insolent that a few such lessons are absolutely necessary to correct them.

Monsieur C—— is a Creole, and belonged to the Staff of the general who commands at Port-au-Prince, from which he has been

E

dismissed in consequence of this affair, which is another proof of the hatred the French offi- cers bear the inhabitants of this country.

We have here a General of division, who is enriching himself by all possible means, and with such unblushing rapacity, that he is universally detested. He was a blacksmith before the revolution, and his present pursuits bear some affinity to his original employment, having taken possession of a plantation on which he makes charcoal, and which he sells to the amount of a hundred dollars a day. A carricature has appeared in which he is repre- sented tying up sacks of coal. Madame A—, his mistress, standing near him, holds up his embroidered coat and says, "Don't soil your- " self, General."

LETTER V.

—

Cape Francois.

Three of your letters arriving at the same time, my dear friend, have made me blush for my impatience, and force me to acknowledge that I have wronged you. But your friendship is so necessary to my happiness that the idea of losing it is insupportable. You know what clouds of misfortune have obscured my life. An orphan without friends, without support, separated from my sister from my infancy, and, at an age when the heart is most alive to tenderness and affection, deprived by the unrelenting hand of death, of him who had taught me to feel all the transports of passion, and for whose loss I felt all its despair—Cast on the world without an asylum, without resource, I met you:—you raised me—soothed me—whispered peace to my lacerated breast!

Ah! can I ever forget that delightful moment when your care saved me? It was so long since I had known sympathy or consolation that my astonished soul knew not how to receive the enchanting visitants; fleeting as fervent was my joy: but let me not repine! Your friendship has shed a ray of light on my solitary way, and though removed from the influence of your immediate presence, I exist only in the hope of seeing you again.

In restoring me to my sister, at the moment of her marriage, you procured for me a home not only respectable, but in which all the charms of fashionable elegance, all the attractions of pleasure are united. Unfortunately, Clara, amidst these intoxicating scenes of ever-varying amusement, and attended by crowds, who offer her the incense of adulation, is wretched, and I cannot be happy!

You know her early habits have been different from mine; affluence might have been thought necessary to her, yet the sensibility of her heart rejects the futile splendour that surrounds her, and the tears that often stain

her brilliant robes, shew that they cover a bosom to which peace is a stranger !

The fortune of her husband was his only
advantage. The friend who had been charged with Clara from her infancy had accustomed her to enjoy the sweets of opulence, and
thought nothing more desirable than to place
her in a situation where she could still command them. Alas her happiness has been the
sacrifice of his mistaken, though well meant,
intentions. St. Louis is too sensible of the
real superiority of his wife not to set some
value on that which he derives from his money, and tears of bitterest regret often fill her
eyes when contemplating the splendor which
has been so dearly purchased. Though to me
he has been invariably kind yet my heart is torn
with regret at the torments which his irascible
temper inflict on his wife. They force her to
seek relief in the paths of pleasure, whilst destined by nature to embellish the sphere of domestic felicity.

LETTER VI.

Cape Francois.

General Rochambeau has given Clara a
proof of his attention to her wishes at once
delicate and flattering. She dined with a large
party at the Government-house, where, as
usual, he was entirely devoted to her. After
dinner, he led her, followed by the company,
to a saloon, that was fitting up for a dining-
room. It was ornamented with military tro-
phies, and on every pannel was written the
name of some distinguished chief.

On one Buonaparte, on another Frederic,
on another Massena, &c.

Clara said it was very pretty, but that
Washington should also have found a place
there!

A few days after, a grand ball was given,

and, on entering the ball-room, we saw, on a pannel facing the door,

Washington, Liberty, and Independence!

This merited a smile, and the general received a most gracious one. It was new-year's eve. When the clock struck twelve, Clara, approaching the general, took a rose from her bosom, saying, let me be the first to wish you a happy new-year, and to offer you les etrennes.

He took the rose, passed it across his lips, and put it in his bosom.

The next morning, an officer called on her, and presented her a pacquet in the name of the general in chief. On opening it she found a brilliant cross, with a superb chain, accompanied by an elegant billet, praying her acceptance of these trifles.

Take it back, she exclaimed, I gave the general a flower, and will accept nothing of greater value.—The officer refused, and, as the eyes of her husband expressed no disapprobation, she kept it.

We have since learned that it is customa-

ry to make at this season, magnificent pre-
sents, and this accounts for the passiveness of
St. Louis on this occasion.

Shortly after, at a breakfast given by Madame A——, Clara appeared with her brilliant cross : the General was there.

When they sat down to table, he offered
her an apple, which she declined accepting.
Take it, said he, for on Mount Ida I would
have given it to you, and in Eden I would
have taken it from you.

She replied laughing, no, no ; since you
attach so much value to your apple I certainly
will not accept it, for I wish equally to avoid
discord and temptation.

Her husband looked displeased, and withdrew as soon as possible.

On their return home, he told her that her
flirting with the General, if carried much farther, would probably cost her too dear. She
became serious, and I foresee the approaching
destruction of all domestic tranquillity.

Clara, proud and high spirited, will submit to no control. If her husband reposed
confidence in her she would not abuse it. But

his soul cannot raise itself to a level with that
of his wife, and he will strive in vain to re-
duce her to that of his own.

He has declared that she shall go to no
more balls; and she has declared as peremp-
torily, that she will go where she pleases. So
on the first public occasion there will be a
contest for supremacy, which will decide forever the empire of the party that conquers.

Their jarrings distress me beyond measure. I had hoped to find tranquillity with
my sister, but alas! she is herself a stranger
to it.

I have no pleasure but that which the recollection of your friendship affords, which
will be dear to my heart whilst that heart is
conscious of feeling or affection.

LETTER VII.

—

Cape Francois.

The brigands have at length made the attack they so long threatened, and we have been terribly alarmed.

On Thursday last, one party approached the fort before day break, whilst another, passing behind the barrier, which is at the entrance of the plain, unobserved by the guard, surprised fort Belleair, which stands on an elevation adjoining the town, and killed the officer and twelve soldiers. The wife of the officer, who commanded that post, had gone, the day before to stay with her husband. Herself and her child were pierced by the same bayonet. The body of the officer lay across the bed, as if he had died in the act of defending them.

The negroes were advancing silently into

the town, when they were discovered by a cen-
tinel who gave the alarm.

The troops rushed to arms. The Brigands
were repulsed : but those who had taken possession of fort Belleair made a vigorous resistance.

St. Louis, who commands a company in the
guarde nationale, was the first on the field.
It was discovered that the negroes in the town
intended to join those who attacked it from
without and to kill the women and children,
who where shut up in their houses, without
any one to defend them ; but the patroles of
the guarde d'honneur prevented, by their vigilance, the execution of this design.

At nine o'clock the general sent to tell
Clara that the part of the town she lived in
being very much exposed, she had better come
to his house and he would send her on board
the admiral's vessel.

She replied that it was impossible for her
to go, her husband having desired her on no
account to leave the house ; therefore she
added, "Here I must stay if I am sure to
perish."

The action continued at the barrier and ad-vanced posts during the day. The negroes, depending on their numbers, seemed deter-mined to decide at once the fate of the town, and we passed the day in a situation which I cannot describe.

In the evening the general sent an officer to tell Clara that he had some news from her husband which he could communicate to none but herself.

The first idea that presented itself was, that St. Louis had been killed. She seized my arm and without waiting to take even a veil hurried out of the house.

A gloomy silence reigned throughout the streets. She arrived breathless at the govern-ment house. The general met her in the hall, took her gravely by the hand and led her into a parlor.

What have you to tell me ? she cried, where is St. Louis ?

Calm your spirits said the general. Your agitation renders you unfit to hear any thing ! But seeing that his hesitation encreased her distress, he said, laughing, your husband is

F

well, has behaved gallantly, and seems invul-
nerable; for though numbers have been killed
and wounded at his post, he has remained un-
hurt!

Then why, she asked, have you alarmed
me so unnecessarily, and made me come here,
when you knew he had desired me not to leave
the house? He will never believe my motive
for coming, and I shall be killed!

The general strove to soothe her, said that
it would be highly improper to pass the night
in her house, that several ladies had embarked, and that she must go on board, which she
positively declined.

At that moment the officer who had accompanied us, entered, and presenting some
papers to the general, they both went into another room.

Directly after the general called Clara.
She went, and I followed her. He was alone,
and looked as if he thought me an intruder,
but I continued at her side.

The papers he held in his hand were dispatches from the camp. He told her that St.
Louis would remain out all night, and again

requested her to think of her own safety.
But she would not listen to his proposal of
sending her on board; and, attended by the officer who had accompanied us, we returned
home.

Whilst the general was talking with Clara,
I examined the apartment, which had been
Madame Le Clerc's dressing-room.

The sofas and curtains were of blue sattin
with silver fringe. A door, which stood open,
led into the bedchamber. The canopy of the
bed was in the form of a shell, from which
little cupids descending held back with one
hand, curtains of white sattin trimmed with
gold, and pointed with the other to a large
mirror which formed the tester. On a table,
in the form of an altar, which stood near the
bed, was an alabaster figure representing silence, with a finger on its lips, and bearing in
its hand a waxen taper.

The first thing we heard on our return
was that a soldier, sent by St. Louis, had enquired for Clara, and not finding her, had returned immediately to the camp.

She was distressed beyond measure, and exclaimed, " I had better go forever, for St. "Louis will kill me!"

I endeavoured to console her, though I felt that her apprehensions were not groundless. She passed the night-in agony, and awaited the return of her husband in the most painful agitation.

At ten the next morning he arrived, having left his post without orders, and thus exposed himself to all the rigours of a court-martial.

He was trembling with rage, transported with fury, and had more the air of a demon than a man.

I know your conduct madam, he cried, on entering, you left the house contrary to my desire; but I shall find means of punishing you, and of covering with shame the monster who has sought to destroy me!

He seized her by the arm, and dragging her into a little dressing-room at the end of the gallery, locked her in, and, taking the key in his pocket, went to the government house, and without waiting till the officers in the antichamber announced him, entered the room where the general was alone, reclining on a sofa, who arose, and approaching him familiarly said, " St. Louis, I am glad to see you, and was just thinking of you ; but did not know that you had been relieved."

I have not been relieved, replied St. Louis, but have left a post where I was most unjustly placed and kept all night, to give you an opportunity of accomplishing your infernal designs. You expected, no doubt, that I would have shared the fate of my brave companions, which I have escaped, and am here to tell you what every body believes but which no body dares utter, that you are a villain !— I know to what I am exposed in consequence of leaving my post. You are my superior, it is true ; but if you are not a coward you will wave all distinction, and give me the satisfaction due to a gentleman you have injured.

He then walked hastily away, before the general could recover from his surprise.

The officer, who had accompanied us the night before, followed and attempted to soothe him.

F 2

He said that he had been sent by the general to take Clara to his house because the
part of the town in which she lived was absolutely unsafe, and that he had used a little
stratagem to induce her to come, but that she
had absolutely refused staying;—that Mademoiselle, (meaning my ladyship) had gone
with her, and that he had not left her till he
had conducted her home.

This a little softened the rage of St. Louis!
He has a good opinion of this young man, who
by the bye, is a charming creature.   They
entered the house together.   I was alone, and
joined my assurances to those of the officer,
that we had not quitted Clara an instant.

He was now sorry for having treated her
so harshly; but did not regret the scene that
had passed at the general's.

At this moment a soldier entered, who told
him that they had been relieved directly after
he had left them, and that no notice had been
taken of his departure.

I now learned that St. Louis, with sixty
men, had been placed in the most advanced
post, on the very summit of the mountain,

where they were crowded together on the point of a rock. In this disadvantageous position, they had been attacked by the negroes; forty men were killed; and the troops of the line, who were a little lower down, had offered them no assistance. It being the first time that the guarde nationale had been placed before the troops of the line the common opinion is, that it was the general's intention to have St. Louis destroyed, as it was by his order that he was so stationed, and kept there all night, though the other posts had been relieved at midnight.

St. Louis forgot his rage and his sufferings in the assurance that Clara had not been faithless. He went to the room in which he had confined her, threw himself at her feet, and burst into tears.

Clara, affected by his pain, or ashamed of having so tormented him,—or fatigued with their eternal broils, leaned over him, and mingled her tears with his.

When the violence of her emotion subsided, she entreated him to forgive the inconsiderateness of her conduct, and vowed that she would never again offend him.—But you have destroyed yourself, she continued, the general will never pardon you : let us leave this hated country, where tranquillity is unknown.

After much debate, it was agreed that he should send us to Philadelphia, and that he would follow himself as soon as he had arranged his affairs.

Clara keeps her room and sees nobody, her husband is in despair at parting with her, but proposes following her immediately.

We embark in ten days. What power shall I invoke to grant us favourable winds? Whose protection solicit to conduct me speedily to my native shores, and to the society of my friends?

LETTER VIII.

Cape Francois.

We are still here, my dear friend, and my disappointment and vexation have been so great, that ten days have passed since I have written a single line.

The general, thinking Clara was sent away against her will, and determined to thwart the intentions of her husband, laid an embargo on all the vessels in the port.

St. Louis raved, and swore she should not leave her room till he conducted her on board.

To prevent all intercourse from without, he keeps her locked up in a small room, adjoining her chamber.—Nobody, not even myself, can see her, except in his presence; and thus all confidence is at an end between them.

She weeps continually, and I am afraid the torments she suffers will destroy her health.

St. Louis is unworthy of her : he thinks it possible to force her to love him :—How much more would a generous confidence influence a heart like her's !

Many of his friends have represented to him the impropriety of his conduct. The challenge he gave general Rochambeau filled every body with terror, for it exposed him to certain death. To have left his post without orders was a crime equally serious ; and, if the general has passed them both over in silence, it is supposed that his vengeance only slumbers for a time to be more sure in its effect.

He thinks Clara attached to the general. I know she is not! her vanity alone has been interested. To be admired was her aim, and she knew that, by attracting the notice of the general in chief, her end would be accomplished. She succeeded even beyond her wishes, but it has been a dangerous experiment ; and will cost her, I fear, the small portion of domestic *peace* she enjoyed.—Domestic *felicity* she never knew ! I am convinced that she has never been less happy than since her marriage!

Nothing can be more brutal than St. Louis in his rage! The day of his affair with the general, he threw her on the ground, and then dragged her by the hair:—I flew to her, but his aspect so terrified me that I was obliged to withdraw: and when his fits of tenderness return he is as bad in the other extreme. He kneels before her, entreats her pardon, and overwhelms her with caresses more painful to her than the most terrible effects of his ill-humour. And then his temper is so capricious that he cannot be counted upon a moment. I have seen him oblige her to stay at home and pass the evening alone with him after she had dressed for a ball.

This does not accord with the liberty French ladies are supposed to enjoy. But I believe Clara is not the first wife that has been locked up at St. Domingo, yet she excites little sympathy because she has not the good fortune to be one of the privileged.

In Continuation.

Certain events, which shall be related, pre-

vented me from finishing my letter. The same
events have produced an entire change in our
affairs, and we are now fixed at St. Domingo
for some time.

The embargo is raised :—the general in
chief is gone to Port-au-Prince ; all the belles
of the Cape have followed him. Clara is at
liberty, and her husband content !

As soon as we had an opportunity of conversing together, Clara related to me occurrences which seem like scenes of romance,
but I am convinced of their reality. Under
the window of the little apartment in which
she was confined, there is an old building
standing in a court surrounded by high walls.
The general informed himself of the position
of Clara's chamber, and his intelligent valet,
who makes love to one of her servants, found
that it would not be difficult to give her a letter, which his dulcinea refused charging herself with. He watched the moment of St.
Louis's absence, entered the deserted court,
mounted the tottering roof, and, calling Clara
to the window, gave her the letter, glowing
with the warmest professions of love, and sug-

gesting several schemes for her escape, one of
which was, that she should embark on board
a vessel that he would indicate, and that he
would agree with the captain to put into Port-
au-Prince, whither he would speedily follow
her.—Another was, to escape in the night by
the same window, and go to his house, where
he would receive and protect her. But the
heart of Clara acknowledged not the empire
of general Rochambeau, nor had she even the
slightest intention of listening to him.

If her husband knew all this it would cure
him, I suppose, of his passion for locking up.
But, incapable of generosity himself, he cannot admire it in another, and would attribute
her refusal of the general's offers to any motive but the real one.

How often has she assured me that she
would prefer the most extreme poverty to her
present existence, but to abandon her husband
was not to be thought of. Yet to have abandoned him, and to have been presented as the
declared mistress of General Rochambeau,
would not have been thought a crime nor have
excluded her from the best society!

Madame G——, who has nothing but her beauty to recommend her, (and no excess of that) lives with the admiral on board his vessel. She is visited by every body ; and no party is thought fashionable if not graced by her presence, yet her manners are those of a poissarde and she was very lately in the lowest and most degraded situation. But she gives splendid entertainments : and when good cheer and gaiety invite, nobody enquires too minutely by whom they are offered.

Clara laughs at the security St. Louis felt when he had her locked up. Yet in spite of bolts and bars love's messenger reached her. The general's letters were most impassioned, for, unaccustomed to find resistance, the difficulty his approach to Clara met added fuel to his flame.

You say, that in relating public affairs, or those of Clara, I forget my own, or conceal them under this appearance of neglect. My fate is so intimately connected with that of my sister, that every thing concerning her must interest you, from the influence it has on myself; and, in truth, I have no adventures. I

described in a former letter, the gallantry of
the French officers, but I have not repeated the
compliments they sometimes make me, and
which have been offered, perhaps, to every
woman in town before they reach my ear.
But a civil thing I heard yesterday, had so
much of originality in it that it deserves to be
remembered. I was copying a beautiful
drawing of the graces, when a Frenchman I
detest, entered the room. Approaching the
table he said. What mademoiselle do you
paint? I did not know that you possessed that
talent. Vexed at his intrusion. I asked if
he knew I possessed any talents. Certainly, he
replied, every body acknowledges that you
possess that of pleasing. Then looking at the
picture that lay before me, he continued : The
modesty of the graces would prevent their attempting to draw you. Why? I asked. Because in painting you, they would be obliged
to copy themselves.

With all this *bavardage* receive my affectionate adieu !

LETTER IX.

———

Cape Francois.

We have had some novelty here my dear
friend, for general Closelle, who commands
during the absence of the general in chief, has
taken a new method to amuse the people, and
courts popularity un er the veil of religion.
He gives no balls, no concerts; but he has had
the church fitted up, and the fete dieu has been
celebrated with great order, magnificence and
solemnity.

At break of day the fete was announced
by the firing of cannon: at eight o'clock the
procession left the church, and passed through
the principal streets, which were strewn with
roses; the fronts of the houses were decorated
with green branches, formed into arches, intermingled with wreaths of flowers. The troops
under arms were placed in double ranks on each

side of the street. The procession was opened
by a number of young boys dressed in white
surplices, singing a hymn in honour of the day.
They were followed by young girls, crowned
with myrtle, bearing in their hands baskets of
flowers, which they strewed on the ground as
they passed along. The band of music followed, and then the priests, bearing golden
censors, in which were burning the most exquisite perfumes, preceded by four negroes,
carrying on their shoulders a golden temple,
ornamented with precious stones, and golden
angels supporting a canopy of crimson velvet,
beneath which the sacred host was exposed in
a brilliant sagraria. After them marched general Closelle, and all the officers of the civil
and military departments. The procession
was closed by a number of ladies, covered with
white veils. As the temple passed along, the
soldiers bent one knee to the ground; and when
it returned to the church, high mass was sung,
accompanied by military music.

Clara and myself, attended by her everlast-
ing beau, major B——, went all over the
town, and so fatigued our poor cavalier, that

he actually fell down; but he is fifty years old, and at least five hundred in constitution; he has been very handsome, has still the finest eyes in the world, is full of anecdote, and infinitely amusing.

General Closelle is very handsome, tall, and elegantly formed, but not at all gallant, consequently not a favourite with the ladies; and for the same reason, a great one with the gentlemen, particularly those who are married. Since the departure of the general in chief he has put every thing on a new footing: the fortifications are repairing, and block-houses are erecting all round the town.

A few days since the negroes attacked a block-house which was nearly finished. A detachment commanded by general Mayart, was instantly sent out to support the guard. As he passed under my window, I told him to hasten and gather fresh laurels. He replied, that at his return he would lay them at my feet; but, alas! he returned no more. The negroes were retreating when he arrived: a random shot struck him, and he fell dead from his horse. This young man came from France

about a year ago, a simple lieutenant; he was
very poor, but being powerfully protected, advanced rapidly in the army; and, what is infinitely surprising, thirty thousand dollars, and a
great quantity of plate, were found in his house
at his death.

Madame G——, a pretty little Parisian,
who was his favourite, is inconsolable. She
faints when any body enters the room, and re-
peats his name in gentle murmurs. In the
evening she languishingly reposes on a sopha
placed opposite the door, and seems to invite
by the gracefulness of her attitudes, and the
negligence of her dress, the whole world to
console her.

The most distressing accounts arrive here
daily from all parts of the island.

The general in chief is at Port-au-Prince,
but he possesses no longer the confidence of
the people. He is entirely governed by his
officers, who are boys, and who think only of
amusement. He gives splendid balls, and elegant parties; but he neglects the army, and
oppresses the inhabitants.

A black chief and his wife were made prisoners last week, and sentenced to be shot.
As they walked to the place of execution the
chief seemed deeply impressed with the horror of his approaching fate: but his wife went
cheerfully along, endeavoured to console him,
and reproached his want of courage. When
they arrived on the field, in which their grave
was already dug, she refused to have her eyes
bound; and turning to the soldiers who were
to execute their sentence, said "Be expedi-
tious, and don't make me linger." She received their fire without shrinking, and expired without uttering a groan. Since the
commencement of the revolution she had been
a very devil! Her husband commanded at St.
Marks, and being very amorously inclined,
every white lady who was unfortunate enough
to attract his notice, received an order to meet
him. If she refused, she was sure of being
destroyed, and if she complied she was as sure
of being killed by his wife's orders, which
were indisputable. Jealous as a tygress, she
watched all the actions of her husband; and
never failed to punish the objects of his amo-

rous approaches, often when they were entirely innocent.

How terrible was the situation of these unfortunate women, insulted by the brutal passion of a negro, and certain of perishing if they
resisted or if they complied.

This same fury in female form killed with
her own hand a white man who had been her
husband's secretary. He offended her; she
had him bound, and stabbed him with a pen-
knife till he expired!

How often, my dear friend, do my sighs
bear my wishes to your happy country; how
ardently do I desire to revisit scenes hallowed
by recollection, and rendered doubly dear by
the peaceful security I there enjoyed, contrast-
ed with the dangers to which we are here exposed. Yet the Creoles still hope; for

" Hope travels through, nor quits us when
we die."

They think it impossible that this island
can ever be abandoned to the negroes. They
build houses, rebuild those that were burned,
and seem secure in their possession. The

measures of general Closelle inspire them with confidence; and they think that if he was commander in chief, all would go well. But when general Rochambeau was second in command, he was a favorite with every body; and it is only since he has attained the summit of power that he has appeared regardless of public opinion! He is said to have the talents of a soldier, but not those of a general. Whatever may be the fate of this country, here I must wait with patience, of which mulish virtue I have no great share, till some change in its affairs restores me to my own. Yet when there, I can hope for nothing more than tranquillity. The romantic visions of happiness I once delighted to indulge in, are fading fast away before the exterminating touch of cold reality.—

The glowing hand of hope grows cold,
And fancy lives not to be old.

But whilst your friendship is left me life will still have a charm.

LETTER X.

—

Cape Francois.

It is not often in the tranquillity of domestic life that the poet or the historian seek their
subjects! Of this I am certain, that in the
calm that now surrounds us it will be difficult
for me to find one for my unpoetical pen.

Clara is dull, St. Louis contented, and I
pass my time heavily, complaining of the fate
which brought me here, and wishing to be
away. We go sometimes to the concerts given
by monsieur d'Or, where madame P——, a
pretty little Parisian sings; and where madame
A——, acccompanied by her daughter, pre-
sides with solemn dignity. This lady, who is
at present a most rigid censor of female conduct, and not amiable either in person or manners, lived many years with monsieur A——,
who raised her from the rank of his house-

H

keeper, to that of his mistress. But he fell in love with another lady, whom he was going to marry. The deserted fair one threw herself in despair at the feet of Toussaint, with whom she had some influence, and so forcibly represented the injustice of the proceeding, that Toussaint ordered A—— to be confined, saying he should not be released till he consented to marry the lady he had so long lived with. A—— resisted some time, but at length yielded, and exchanged his prison for the softer one of her arms.

Before the revolution there was a convent at the Cape. The nuns in general were very rich, and devoted themselves chiefly to the education of young ladies: some of their pupils, I have heard, would have done honour to a Parisian seminary.

When religion was abolished in France, the rage for abolition, as well as that of revolutionizing reached this place, and the nuns were driven from the convent by Santhonax, a name which will always fill every Frenchman's breast with horror: he caused the first destruction of the Cape. On the arrival of ge-

neral Galbo, who was sent to supercede him,
he said, "if Galbo reigns here, he shall reign
over ashes," and actually set fire to the town.
The convent was not then burned; but the
society was dissolved, the habit of the order
laid aside; and some of the nuns, profiting by
the license of the times, married. One of
these became the wife of a man who, during
the reign of the negroes committed crimes of
the deepest die. He has not yet received the
punishment due to them; but he awaits in
trembling the hour of retribution. I often see
her. She has been very handsome, but her
charms are now in the wane; she has a great
deal of vivacity, and that fluency of expression
in conversing on the topics of the day, which
gives to a French woman the reputation of
having *beaucoup d'esprit.*

I know also the lady abbess, who is an
excellent woman of most engaging manners.
She lives in a miserable chamber, and sup-
ports herself by her industry. The greatest
part of the community have perished; and general Le Clerc found it more convenient to
have the convent fitted up for his own resi-

dence, than to restore it to its owners, the government house having been entirely destroyed.

There are also here two hospitals, neither of which have been injured, though the town has been twice burned. The *Hopitale de la Providence* is an asylum for the poor, the sick and the stranger; the building is decent: but the *Hopitale des Peres de la Charite* is superb, surrounded by gardens, ornamented with statues and fountains, and finished with all the magnificence which their vast revenues enabled its owners to command.

The streets of the town cross each other at right angles, like those of Philadelphia, and there are several public squares which add greatly to the beauty of the place. In the centre of each is a fountain, from which the water, clear as crystal, flows into marble basons. The houses are commodious, particularly those of two stories, which have all balconies; but the streets are narrow, and the heat would be intolerable if it was not for the relief afforded by bathing, which is here an universal custom, and for the sea-breezes which, rising every afternoon, waft on their wings delicious coolness.

The mulatto women are the hated but successful rivals of the Creole ladies. Many of them are extremely beautiful; and, being destined from their birth to a life of pleasure, they are taught to heighten the power of their charms by all the aids of art, and to express in every look and gesture all the refinements of voluptuousness. It may be said of them, that their very feet speak. In this country that unfortunate class of beings, so numerous in my own,—victims of seduction, devoted to public contempt and universal scorn, is unknown. Here a false step is very rarely made by an unmarried lady, and a married lady, who does not make one, is as rare; yet of both there have been instances: but the *faux pas* of a married lady is so much a matter of course, that she who has only one lover, and retains him long in her chains, is considered as a model of constancy and discretion.

To the destiny of the women of colour no infamy is attached; they have inspired passions which have lasted through life, and are

faithful to their lovers through every vicissi-
tude of fortune and chance. But before the
revolution their splendor, their elegance, their
influence over the men, and the fortunes lavished on them by their infatuated lovers, so
powerfully excited the jealousy of the white
ladies, that they complained to the council of
the ruin their extravagance occasioned to many
families, and a decree was issued imposing re-
strictions on their dress. No woman of colour was to wear silk, which was then universally worn, nor to appear in public without a
handkerchief on her head. They determined
to oppose this tyranny, and took for that purpose a singular but effectual resolution. They
shut themselves up in their houses, and appeared no more in public. The merchants
soon felt the bad effects of this determination,
and represented so forcibly the injury the decree did to commerce, that it was reversed,
and the olive beauties triumphed.

But the rage of the white ladies still pur-
sued them with redoubled fury, for what is so
violent as female jealousy? The contest however was unequal, and the influence of their

detested rivals could not be counteracted. Some of them were very rich. There is a friendliness and simplicity in their manners which is very interesting. They are the most caressing creatures in the world, and breathe nothing but affection and love. One of their most enviable privileges, and which they inherit from nature, is that their beauty is immortal—they never fade.

The French appear to understand less than any other people the delights arising from an union of hearts. They seek only the gratification of their sensual appetites. They gather the flowers, but taste not the fruits of love. They call women the " *beau sexe*," and know them only under the enchanting form of ministers of pleasure. They may appear thus to those who have only eyes; by those who have hearts they will always be considered as sacred objects of reverence and love. A man who thinks and feels views in woman the beneficent creature who nourished him with her milk, and watched over his helpless infancy; a consoling being who soothes his pains and softens his sorrows by her tenderness and even

by her levity and her sports. But here female
virtue is blasted in the bud by the contagious
influence of example.   Every girl sighs to be
married to escape from the restraint in which
she is held whilst single, and to enjoy the un-
bounded liberty she so often sees abused by
her mother.   A husband is necessary to give
her a place in society; but is considered of so
little importance to her happiness, that in the
choice of one her inclination is very seldom
consulted.   And when her heart, in spite of
custom, feels the pain of being alone, and
seeks an asylum in the bosom of her husband,
she too often finds it shut against her; she is
assailed by those whose only desire is to add
another trophy to their conquests, and is borne
away by the torrent of fashion and dissipation
till all traces of her native simplicity are destroyed.   She joins with unblushing front, the
crowd who talk of sentiments they never feel,
and who indulge in the most licentious excesses without having the glow of passion to
gild their errors.   These reflections were sug-
gested by a most preposterous marriage, at
which I was present.   A girl of fifteen was sa-

crificed by her grandmother to a man of sixty, of the most disagreeable appearance and forbidding manners. The soul of this unfortunate victim is all melting softness; she is of the most extraordinary beauty; she is now given to the world, and in those who surround her she will find the destroyers of her delicacy, her simplicity, and her peace.

LETTER XI.

———

Cape Francois.

To give you some idea of the despotism
that reigns in this country, I must relate an
event which, though it originated with Clara,
was certainly carried farther than she either
expected or desired.

On our arrival here she engaged a young
Frenchman to give her lessons in his language,
which she spoke tolerably before, but in which
she wished to acquire perfection. After he
had attended her some time she perceived that
his lessons were considerably lengthened and
that he chose for his themes the most amorous
and affectionate pieces. Some observations
made on the subject, drew from him a confes-
sion of the extraordinary passion she had inspired. After laughing at his folly, she dis-

missed him, and thought of him no more; but shortly after was informed that he had circulated reports highly injurious to her. General Rochambeau, whose ears they had reached, asked her from whence they arose? and she related to him with great simplicity the whole affair. The general said he should be embarked, and the next morning he was actually sent on board an armed vessel which was to sail in a few days. Whilst there he wrote a pathetic and elegant little poem in which he represented himself as the victim of the general's jealousy, who thus sought to destroy him for having interfered, and not unsuccessfully, with his pursuits. This paper was sent to the man with whom he had lived, and who handed it to every body. Clara was in despair. She informed the general in chief that he had rendered the affair, which was at first only ridiculous, seriously provoking: in consequence of which the house of this man was surrounded by guards, who, without giving him time to take even a change of clothes, conducted him on board the vessel where his friend was confined; it sailed immediately for France, and his house and store, which were worth at least thirty thousand dollars became the prey of the officers of the administration: but the poem was heard of no more.

LETTER XII.

———

Cape Francois.

The general in chief has returned from
Port-au-Prince. Three days after his arrival
the Cape was blockaded by five British ships,
and news was received of war having been
declared between England and France.

Every body is in the greatest consternation, for inevitable ruin threatens the place.
The English will no doubt prevent all vessels
from entering the port, and take all that go
out; at the same time the negroes are said to
be preparing another attack.

The general brought in his train all the
belles of Port-au-Prince, and has given a ball,
at which, incredible as it may appear to you,
Clara and myself appeared. When the cards
of invitation were brought, St. Louis declared
that they should not be left; but major B——,

who was present, represented so forcibly the danger of irritating the general, who has shewn some symptoms of a disposition to tyrannize, since his return which were never remarked in him before, that he consented to our going. When we entered the room attended by B, every eye was fixed on Clara, who never was so lovely. Dressed in a robe ornamented with wreaths of flowers, she joined the sweetness of Flora to the lightness of the youngest of the graces, and the recollection of certain late events gave an air of timidity to her looks which rendered her enchanting. General Rochambeau, by the warmth of his manner encreased her confusion, and fixed on her more pointedly the attention of every beholder. He was surprized at seeing her without her husband, and enquired what had wrought so wonderful a change? She replied that he had found a very good representative in major B——, and that he had acquired a little confidence in herself. She waltzed with more than her usual grace, and the general seemed flattered by the notice she attracted.

Most of the ladies from Port-au-Prince
are widows

" Who bear about the mockery of woe
To midnight dances and the public shew."

None of them are remarkable for their beauty
or elegance. The only new face worth looking at was a madame V——, lately arrived
from France; her hair was dressed *a la Ninon
de l'Enclos*, part of it fastened on the top of
the head, the rest hanging about her neck in
loose curls.

The ball room had been newly furnished
with regal splendor; all the chairs were removed, and long sophas with large cushions
offered delightful seats. A recess at one end
of the room had been fitted up *a la Turc*; the
walls were entirely concealed with large looking glasses, which reached the ceiling; the
floor was covered with carpets and the only
seats were piles of crimson sattin cushions
thrown on the ground. The lustres, veiled
with green silk, gave a soft light, imitating that
of the moon, and the *ensemble* breathed an air
of tranquillity that invited to repose after the

fatigue of dancing, and offered a retreat from
the heat which it was almost impossible to resist. To this retreat general Rochambeau led
Clara.   A lady was lolling in one corner, and
I entered at the same moment. He looked as
if he wished us both away, but I never attend
to looks that I am resolved not to understand.

LETTER XIII.

Cape Francois.

A few days after the ball mentioned in my last, St. Louis determined to send Clara and myself to St. Jago de Cuba, and to follow us as soon as possible. This measure was opposed by major B——; but Clara insisted, and the day of our departure was fixed. The next day B—— breakfasted with us; and as soon as we were alone, told Clara that she was wrong in being so entirely governed by her husband. She replied, that she had suffered much in consequence of coquetting with general Rochambeau, in which her only intention had been to find amusement; but she was now convinced of its being highly dangerous and improper; and that it had been productive of much ill. She added, that she lived in continual inquietude, and that nothing would induce her to stay in the Cape if she could get away.

B—— spoke of the passion of the general, —said he had seen him that morning, and as a proof of her having been the subject of their conversation, gave her a letter from him. Is it possible, (she exclaimed) you in whom my husband has so much confidence? You are a fool, replied B——, and your husband is no better: and if his insolence to the general has not been punished it is owing to my interference.

Clara read the letter. It was filled with professions of admiration and unalterable love. He begged her not to think of leaving the Cape, which was in no danger; and further said he had taken measures to prevent her being sent away. He requested her to write to him, but this she positively refused.

Towards noon a proclamation was issued ordering all the passports which had been granted during the last three months to be returned. St. Louis was in despair: he had intended sending Clara off without eclat, having procured passports before, but B—— betray-

ed him.   Yet in B—— he has the most un-
bounded confidence; and suffers Clara to receive nobody else.   She walks with him when
she pleases, and he never fails on such occa-
sions to give the general an opportunity of
speaking to her.

A few days ago we went to Picolet, to see
the fort.   The road to it winds along the sea-
shore at the foot of the mountain.   The rocks
are covered with the Arabian jessamin, which
grows here in the greatest profusion.   Its flex-
ible branches form among the cliffs moving
festoons and fantastic ornaments, and its flowers
whiter than snow, fill the air with intoxicating
fragrance.   After having visited the fort we
were preparing to return, when we saw a troop
of horsemen descending the mountain.   They
came full speed.   We soon discovered they
were the general and his suite; and as they
followed the windings of the road, with their
uniform *a la mameluc*, and their long sabres,
they appeared like a horde of Arabs.

The general arrived first, and jumping from
his horse, told Clara that he had left the table
an hour sooner than usual to have the plea-

sure of seeing her. Then, said she, looking
reproachfully at B——, you have a familiar
spirit who informs you of my movements!
Why not, he replied, are you not an enchan-
tress, and have you not employed all the
powers of magic to enslave me ? You are in
an error said Clara ; I was flattered by your
admiration, and gratified by the attentions with
which you honoured me; but I used no art to
attract the one, and am too sensible of my own
defects not to feel that I am indebted for the
other entirely to your goodness. That is too
modest to be natural, cried the general. Nobody who possesses your charms can be ignorant of their power; nor could any one mistake the passion I have evinced for you, for
the common attention every lady receives as
her due. Then you do not believe a woman
can be modest? asked Clara. Modest if you
please, but not insensible, he replied. And
suffer me to observe,——Oh no observations,
I entreat, interrupted Clara; for this interview
will, I fear, occasion too many.——But tell me,
how did you learn I was to be here; and why
have you left the table where you so often sa-

crifice till a late hour to the rosy god, to wander among these rugged rocks where despairing lovers alone would seek a retreat? And are you of that number? he enquired. No, she replied: but I have not your motives for staying at home: I was led here by curiosity; It is my first visit to this spot. Then believe, said the general, that I came here to offer at your feet that homage which envious fate has hitherto deprived me of an opportunity of paying. During this conversation, he had drawn her to a point of the rock; and the officers of his suite, surrounding me, sought to divert my attention by all the common place compliments of which they are so profuse. I had forgotten Clara for a moment, when, turning, I beheld the general, who bending one knee to the ground, seized her hand passionately, and at the same time I saw St. Louis ascending the mountain.

Pressing through the crowd I flew to her, saying, are you mad? Rise general, for heaven's sake! her husband approaches! what means this exhibition of folly? Yes I am mad, he replied, I adore your sister, and she refuses to

listen to me. My sister is married, I answered. But, said he, she loves not her husband.
At least I love no one more than him, said
Clara, trembling at the idea of having been
seen by St. Louis. Fortunately I had discovered him at the foot of the mountain, and the
road winds round its base with so many turn-
ings that it is of considerable length and before he arrived she was tolerably composed.

You have deceived me, said the general.
I never listened to you, she replied. But you
have read my letters.—I could not avoid receiving, but I never answered them. Still, he
observed, interrupting her, I will hope; for
your eyes cannot utter falsehood, and from
them I have received encouragement.

At that instant St. Louis arrived; he appeared astonished at seeing Clara so surrounded, and advancing involuntarily, as if to defend
her, took her arm.

The general, with his usual levity, told St.
Louis, that he came in time to prevent him
from running away with his wife. Then twin-
ing round her arm a wreath of jessamin he had
taken from my hand, said, with such fetters

only you should be bound! Does she find those that bind her too heavy? asked her husband. No, replied the general, she seems content. Then casting a look of disappointment at Clara, he mounted his horse and rode off.

Major B—— engaged St. Louis in a conversation on the situation of the colony, which made him forget the dangerous one in which he had found his wife.

Clara, leaning on my arm, seemed oppressed by a variety of sensations, among which indignation predominated. The security and presumption of the general shocked her, and the recollection of having, at least negatively encouraged him, gave an additional pang to her heart. We returned slowly home. Our meeting with general Rochambeau was thought accidental by St. Louis, and was taken no notice of.

LETTER XIV.

Cape Francois.

Ah, my dear friend, where shall I find expressions to convey to you an idea of the horror that fills my soul; how describe scenes at which I tremble even now with terror?

Three negroes were caught setting fire to a plantation near the town. They were sentenced to be burnt alive; and the sentence was actually executed. When they were tied to the stake and the fire kindled, one of them, I understand, held his head over the smoke and was suffocated immediately. The second made horrible contortions, and howled dreadfully. The third, looking at him comtemptuously said, Peace! do you not know how to die? and preserved an unalterable firmness till the devouring flames consumed him. This cruel act has been blamed by every body, as giving a bad example to the negroes, who will not fail to retaliate on the first prisoners they take. But it has been succeeded by a deed which has absolutely chilled the hearts of the people. Every one trembles for his own safety, and silent horror reigns throughout the place.

A young Creole, who united to the greatest elegance of person the most polished manners and the most undaunted courage, had incurred, I know not how, the displeasure of general Rochambeau, and had received a hint of approaching danger, but neither knew what he had to fear, nor how to avoid it, when he received an order to pay into the treasury, before three o'clock, twenty thousand dollars on pain of death. This was at ten in the morning. He thought at first it was a jest; but when assured that the order was serious, said he would rather die than submit to such injustice, and was conducted by a guard to prison. Some of his friends went to the government-house to intercede for him. Nobody was admitted. His brother exerted himself to raise the sum required; but though their house has a great deal of property, and government is indebted to them more than a hundred thousand dollars, it was difficult, from the scarcity of cash, to raise so large a sum in so short a time, and nobody thought there was any danger to be apprehended. At half after two o'clock he was taken to the fosset, where his grave was already dug. The captain of the guard sent to know if there was no reprieve: and was told that there was none. He sent again, the same answer was returned, with an order to perform his duty, or his life would be the forfeit of his disobedience. He was a Creole, the friend, the companion of the unfortunate Feydon. Ah! how could he submit to be the vile instrument of tyranny? how could he sacrifice his friend? Why did he not resign his commission on the spot, and abide by the consequence? Approaching Feydon, he offered to bind his eyes; but he refused, saying, No, let me witness your horrors to the last moment. He was placed on the brink of his grave. They fired: he fell! but from the bottom of his grave cried, I am

K 2

not dead—finish me! My heart bleeds: I knew him; and while I live, the impression this dreadful event has made on me will never be effaced. At the moment he was killed his brother, having collected the required sum, carried it to the general, who took the money, and sent the young man, who was frantic when he heard of his brother's fate, to prison. It is said a reprieve had been granted, but had been suppressed by Nero the commandant de la place, who is as cruel, and as much detested as was the tyrant whose name he bears.

A few days after, nine of the principal merchants were selected. One hundred thousand dollars was the sum demanded from them; and they were imprisoned till it should be found. It was then the virtuous Leaumont approached, fearless of consequences, the retreat of the tyrant, and obliged him to listen to the voice of truth. He represented the impossibility of finding the sum demanded from these unfortunate men, and entreated to have a tax laid on every individual of the place in proportion to his property, which, after much debate was consented to. The money was soon furnished, and the prisoners released.

Since the death of Feydon the general appears no more in public. A settled gloom pervades the place, and every one trembles lest he should be the next victim of a monster from whose power there is no retreat. St. Louis, above all, is in the greatest danger, for he has the reputation of being rich, and, having excited the aversion of general Rochambeau, it is not probable that he will escape without some proof of his animosity.

Clara is in the greatest dejection. She repents bitterly the levity of her conduct, and is torn with anxiety for the fate of her husband. She loves him not, it is true, but would be in despair if through her fault the least evil befel him, and feels for the first time the danger of awakening the passions of those who are capable of sacrificing all considerations to gratify their wishes or revenge their disappointment. She requested the general to give her a passport for St. Jago de Cuba. He replied that he could only grant them to the old and ugly, and she, not being of this description, he was obliged to refuse her; however, after much solicitation, she obtained one for herself for me and her servants, and we shall sail in a few days. All the women are suffered to depart, but no man can procure a passport. Some it is true, find means to escape in disguise, and they are fortunate, for it is much feared that those who remain will be sacrificed. Every vessel that sails from hence is seized and plundered by the English; but, as we are Americans, perhaps we may pass.

Our intention is to stay at St. Jago till St. Louis joins us. God knows whether we shall ever see him again. With what joy I shall leave this land of oppression! how much that joy would be increased if I was going to the continent; but in all places, and in all countries I shall be affectionately yours.

LETTER XV.

Barracoa.

You will no doubt be surprised at receiving a letter from hence, but here we are my
dear friend, deprived of every thing we possessed, in a strange country, of whose language we are ignorant, and where, even with
money, it would be impossible to procure what
we have been accustomed to consider as the
necessaries of life.   Yet here we have found
an asylum, and met with sympathy; not that
of words, but active and effectual sympathy,
from strangers, which, perhaps, we should
have sought in vain in our own country, and
among our own people.

   We embarked at the Cape, Clara, myself
and six servants, in a small schooner, which
was full of women, and bound to St. Jago.
As soon as we were out of the harbour a boat

from a British frigate boarded us, condemned
the vessel as French property, and, without
further ceremony, sent the passengers on board
another vessel which was lying near us, and
was going to Barracoa, where we arrived in
three days, after having suffered much from
want of provisions and water. Every thing
belonging to us had been left in the schooner
the English made a prize of St. Louis, having forseen the probability of tnis event, had
made Clara conceal fifty doubloons in her
corset.

On our arrival at Barracoa, a Frenchman
we had known at the Cape came on board.
He conducted us ashore, and procured us a
room in a miserable hut, where we passed the
night on a board laid on the ground, it being
impossible to procure a mattrass. The next
morning the first consideration was clothes.
There was not a pair of shoes to be found in
the place, nor any thing which we would have
thought of employing for our use if we had
not been obliged by the pressure of necessity.
Clara had given a corner of our hut to a lady

who, with two children, was without a shilling.

While we were at breakfast, which we
made of chocolate, served in little calabashes,
lent us by the people of the house, a priest of
most benign aspect entered, and addressing
Clara in French, which he speaks fluently, told
her that having heard of our arrival and misfortunes, he had come to offer his services,
and enquired how we had passed the night?
Clara shewed him the boards on which we had
slept. He rose instantly, and calling the mistress of the house, spoke to her angrily. I
afterwards learned that he reproached her for
not having informed him of our distress as soon
as we arrived. He took his leave and returned
in half an hour with three or four negroes who
brought mattrasses, and baskets filled with
fowls, and every kind of fruit the island pro-
duces. Then, telling Clara that his sister
would call on her in the evening, and begging
her to consider him as her servant, and every
thing he possessed at her disposal, he went
away. In the afternoon he returned with his
sister. She is a widow. Her manners are in-

teresting, but she speaks no language except
her own, of which not one of us understood a
word.

Father Philip sent for the only shopkeeper
in the place, who furnished us with black silk
for dresses, and some miserable linen. By
the next day we were decently equipped. We
were then presented to the governor, whose
wife is divinely beautiful. Nothing can equal
the lustre of her eyes, or surpass the fascinating power of her graceful and enchanting manners. The changes of her charming countenance express every emotion of her soul, and
she seems not to require the aid of words to
be understood. She conceived at once a fervent friendship for Clara, and having learned
our misfortunes from father Philip, insisted on
our living in her house whilst we remained at
Barracoa. This point was disputed by Donna Angelica, who said she had provided a
chamber for us in her own. But madame la
Governadora was not to be thwarted; she
seized Clara by the arm, and drawing her
playfully into another room, insisted on dress-
ing her *a la Espagnole*, which is nothing more

than a cambric *chemise*, cut very low in the bosom, an under petticoat of linen, made very stiff with starch, and a muslin one over it, both very short. To this is added, when they go out, a large black silk veil, which covers the head and falls below the waist. By this dress the beauty of the bosom, which is so carefully preserved by the French is lost.

Clara looked very well in this costume, but felt uncomfortable. As Donna Jacinta would not hear of our leaving her we consented to stay; and a chamber was prepared for us. In the evening we walked through the town, and were surprised to see such extreme want in this abode of hospitality. The houses are built of twigs, interwoven like basket work, and slightly thatched with the leaves of the palm tree, with no other floor than the earth. The inhabitants sit on the ground, and eat altogether out of the pot in which their food is prepared. Their bed is formed of a dried hide, and they have no clothes but what they wear, nor ever think of procuring any till these are in rags.

L

There are only three decent houses in the place, which belong to the governor, to father Philip, and his sister ; yet these good people are happy, for they are contented. Their poverty is not rendered hideous by the contrast of insolent pride or unfeeling luxury. They dose away their lives in a peaceful obscurity, which if I do not envy, I cannot despise. There are many French families here from St. Domingo; some almost without resource; and this place offers none for talents of any kind. It is not uncommon to hear the sound of a harp or piano from beneath a straw built shed, or to be arrested by a celestial voice issuing from a hut which would be supposed uninhabitable.

Clara studies with so much application the Spanish language that she can already hold with tolerable ease a conversation, especially with the seignora Jacinta, whose eyes are so eloquent that it would be impossible not to understand her. She is a native of the Havanna, was married very young, and her husband having been appointed governor of Barracoa,

was obliged to leave the gaiety and splendour
of her native place for this deserted spot,
where fashion, taste or elegance had never
been known.   It has been a little enlivened
since the misfortunes of the French have
forced them to seek in it a retreat.

Jacinta has too much sensibility not to regret the change of situation; but she never re-
pines, and seeks to diffuse around her the
cheerfulness by which she is animated. From
early prejudice she loves not the French character.   Fortunately Clara is an American;
and the influence of her enchanting qualities
on the heart of her fair friend is strengthened
by the charm of novelty.

We are waiting for a vessel to carry us to
St. Jago, and its arrival, I assure you will fill
us with regret.

LETTER XVI.

St. Jago de Cuba.

We have left Barracoa, the good Father
Philip, his generous sister, and the beautiful
Jacinta. Removed from them for ever, the
recollection of their goodness will accompany
me through life, and a sigh for the peaceful
solitude of their retreat will often heave my
breast amid the mingled scenes of pleasure
and vexation in which I shall be again engaged. Fortunate people! who, instead of ram-
bling about the world, end their lives beneath
the roofs where they first drew breath. Fortunate in knowing nothing beyond their horizon; for whom even the next town is a strange
country, and who find their happiness in con-
tributing to that of those who surround them!
The wife of the governor could not separate
herself from us. Taking from her neck a ro-

sary of pearls, she put it round that of Clara,
pressed her in her arms, wept on her bosom,
and said she never passed a moment so painful. She is young, her soul is all tenderness
and ardour, and Clara has filled her breast
with feelings to which till now she has been a
stranger. Her husband is a good man, but
without energy or vivacity, the direct reverse
of his charming wife She can never have
awakened an attachment more lively than the
calmest friendship. She has no children, nor
any being around her, whose soul is in unison
with her own. With what devotion she would
love! but if a stranger to the exquisite pleasures of that sentiment she is also ignorant of
its pains! may no destructive passion ever
trouble her repose.

She walked with us to the shore and waited
on the beach till we embarked. She shrieked
with agony when she clasped Clara for the last
time to her breast, and leaning against a tree,
gave unrestrained course to her tears.

The good father Philip accompanied us
to the vessel, and staid till the moment of our
departure. He had previously sent aboard

every thing that he thought would be agreeable to us during the voyage. His friendly soul poured itself forth in wishes for our happiness. May all the blessings of heaven be showered on his head!

It is Clara's fate to inspire great passions. Nobody loves her moderately. As soon as she is known she seizes on the soul, and centres every desire in that of pleasing her. The friendship she felt for Jacinta, and the impression father Philip's goodness made on her, rendered her insensible to all around her.

The vessel was full of passengers, most of them ladies, who were astonished at beholding such grief. One of them, a native of Jeremie, was the first who attracted the attention of Clara. This lady, who is very handsome, and very young, has three children of the greatest beauty, for whom she has the most impassioned fondness, and seems to view in them her own protracted existence. She has all the bloom of youth, and when surrounded by her children, no picture of Venus with the loves and graces was ever half so interesting. She is going to join her husband at St. Jago, who

I hear, is a great libertine, and not sensible of
her worth.   An air of sadness dwells on her
lovely countenance, occasioned, no doubt, by
his neglect and the pain of finding a rival in
every woman he meets.

There is also on board a beautiful widow
whose husband was killed by the negroes, and
who, without fortune or protection, is going
to seek at St. Jago a subsistence, by employing her talents.   There is something incon-
ceivably interesting in these ladies.   Young,
beautiful, and destitute of all resource, supporting with cheerfulness their wayward for
tune.

But the most captivating trait in their
character is their fondness for their children!
The Creole ladies, marrying very young, appear more like the sisters than the mothers of
their daughters.   Unfortunately they grow up
too soon, and not unfrequently become the
rivals of their mothers.

We are still on board, at the entrance of
the harbour of St. Jago, which is guarded by
a fort, the most picturesque object I ever saw.
It is built on a rock that hangs over the sea,

and the palm trees which wave their lofty,
heads over its ramparts, add to its beauty.

We are obliged to wait here till to-mor-
row; for this day being the festival of a saint,
all the offices are shut. No business is trans-
acted, and no vessel can approach the town
without permission.

This delay is painful; I am on the wing
to leave the vessel, though it is only four days
since we left Barracoa.—I wish to know whether we shall meet as much hospitality here as
in that solitary place. Yet why should I expect it? Hearts like those of father Philip
and the lovely Jacinta do not abound.—How
many are there who, never having witnessed
such goodness, doubt its existence?

We have letters to several families here,
from the governor of Barracoa and father Philip, and St. Louis has friends who have been
long established at this place. Therefore, on
arriving, we shall feel at home; perhaps too,
we may find letters from the Cape;—God
grant they may contain satisfactory intelligence.

LETTER XVII.

St. Jago de Cuba.

A month has passed, since our arrival in
this place, in such a round of visits and such
a variety of amusements, that I am afraid, my
dear friend, you will think I have forgotten
you. We were received by the gentleman,
to whom Clara was directed, with the most
cordial friendship. He is an ancient Cheva-
lier de St. Louis, and retains, with much of
the formality of the court of France, at which
he was raised, all its elegance and urbanity;
and having lived a number of years in this
island, he is loved and respected by all its in-
habitantss.

The letters which father Philip and the
governor of Barracoa gave us to their friends,
have procured us great attention.

The people here are much the same as at

Barracoa; perhaps they are a little more civi-
lized. There is some wealth, with much poverty. The women have made great progress
towards improvement since such numbers of
French have arrived from St. Domingo.—
They are at least a century before the men in
refinement, but women are every where more
susceptible of polish than the lords of the cre-
ation. Those of this town are not generally
remarkable for their beauty. There are some,
however, who would be admired even in Philadelphia, particularly the wife of the governor;
but they are all remarkable for the smallness
of their feet, and they dress their hair with a
degree of taste in which they could not be ex-
celled by the ladies of Paris.

We arrived in the season of gaiety, and
have been at several balls; but their balls
please me not!—Every body in the room dances a minuet, which you may suppose is tedious enough; then follow the country dances,
which resemble the English, except that they
are more complicated and more fatiguing.

There are in this town eleven churches,
all of them splendid, and the number of priests

is incredible ! Many of them may be ranked among the most worthless members of the community. It is not at all uncommon to see them drunk in the street, or to hear of their having committed the most shocking excesses. Some, however, are excellent men, who do honour to their order and to human nature. But the thickest veil of superstition covers the land, and it is rendered more impervious by the clouds of ignorance in which the people are enveloped !

Clara, who speaks the language with the facility of a native, asked some of her Spanish friends for books, but there was not one to be found in the place. She complained some days ago of a head-ache, and a Spanish lady gave her a ribbon, which had been bound round the head of an image of the Virgin telling her it was a sovereign remedy for all pains of the head.

The bishop is a very young man and very handsome. We see him often at church, where we go, attracted by the music. But one abominable custom observed there, destroys our pleasure. The women kneel on

M

carpets, spread on the ground, and when they are fatigued, cross their legs, and sit Turkish fashion ; whilst the men loll at their ease on sofas. From whence this subversion of the general order ? Why are the women placed in the churches at the feet of their slaves ?

The lower classes of the people are the greatest thieves in the world, and they steal with so much dexterity, that it is quite a science. The windows are not glazed, but secured by wooden bars, placed very close together. The Spaniards introduce between these bars long poles, which have at one end a hook of iron, and thus steal every thing in the room, even the sheets off the beds. The friars excel in this practice, and conceal their booty in their large sleeves !

In the best houses and most wealthy families there is a contrast of splendour and poverty which is shocking. Their beds and furniture are covered with a profusion of gilding and clumsy ornaments, while the slaves, who serve in the family, and even those who are about the persons of the ladies, are in rags and filthy to the most disgusting degree !

How different were the customs of St. Domingo! The slaves, who served in the houses, were dressed with the most scrupulous neatness, and nothing ever met the eye that could occasion an unpleasant idea.

The Spanish women are sprightly, and devoted to intrigue. Their assignations are usually made at church. The processions at night, and the masses celebrated before daylight, are very favourable to the completion of their wishes, to which also their dress is well adapted. They wear a black silk petticoat; their head is covered with a veil of the same colour, that falls below the waist; and, this costume being universal, and never changed, it is difficult to distinguish one woman from another. A man may pass his own wife in the street without knowing her. Their attachments are merely sensual. They are equally strangers to the delicacy of affection or that refinement of passion which can make any sacrifice the happiness of its object may require.

To the licentiousness of the people, more than to their extreme poverty, may be attributed the number of children which are con tinually exposed to perish in the street. Almost every morning, at the door of one of the churches, and often at more than one, a new-born infant is found. There is an hospital, where they are received, but those who find them, are (if so disposed,) at liberty to keep them. The unfortunate little beings who happen to fall into the hands of the lower classes of the people, increase, during their childhood, the throng of beggars, and augment, as they grow up, the number of thieves.

The heart recoils at the barbarity of a mother who can thus abandon her child; but the custom, here, as in China, is sanctioned by habit and excites no horror!

LETTER XVIII.

St. Jago de Cuba.

We have received no news from the Cape, my dear friend, but it is generally expected that it will be evacuated, as several parts of the island have been already.

This place is full of the inhabitants of that unfortunate country, and the story of every family would offer an interesting and pathetic subject to the pen of the novelist.

All have been enveloped in the same terrible fate, but with different circumstances; all have suffered, but the sufferings of each individual derive their hue from the disposition of his mind.

One catastrophe, which I witnessed, is dreadfully impressive! I saw youth, beauty and affection sink to an untimely grave, with-

M 2

out having the power of softening the bitterness of their fate.

Madame C——, a native of Jeremie, had
been sent by her husband to Philadelphia, at
the beginning of the revolution, where she
continued several years, devoting all her time
to improving the mind and cultivating the talents of her only child, the beautiful Clarissa.

Sometime after the arrival of the French
fleet, Madame C——, and her daughter returned to Jeremie. She had still all the charms
of beauty, all the bloom of youth. She was
received by her husband with a want of tenderness which chilled her heart, and she soon
learned that he was attached to a woman of
colour on whom he lavished all his property.
This, you may suppose, was a source of mor-
tification to Madame C——, but she suffered in silence, and sought consolation in the
bosom of her daughter.

When the troubles of Jeremie encreased,
and it was expected every day that it would
be evacuated, Monsieur C—— resolved to
remove to St. Jago de Cuba. He sent his wife
and child in one vessel, and embarked with

his mistress in another. Arriving nearly at the
same time, he took a house in the country, to
which he retired with his superannuated favourite, leaving his family in town, and in
such distress that they were often in want of
bread.

Madame C———, too delicate to expose
the conduct of her husband, or to complain,
concealed from her friends her wants and her
grief.

A young Frenchman was deeply in love
with her daughter, but his fortune had been
lost in the general wreck, and he had nothing
to offer to the object of his adoration except a
heart glowing with tenderness. He made Madame C.— the confidant of his affection. She
was sensible of his worth, and would willingly
have made him the protector of her daughter,
had she not been struggling herself with all
the horrors of poverty and therefore thought
it wrong to encourage his passion.

He addressed himself to her father, and
this father was rich!   He lavished on his mistress all the comforts and elegancies of life,
yet refused to his family the scantiest pittance!

He replied to the proposal that his daughter might marry, but that it was impossible for him to give her a shilling.

Clarissa heard the unfeeling sentence with calm despair. She had just reached the age in which the affections of the heart develope themselves. The beauty of her form was un-equalled, and innocence, candour, modesty, generosity, and heroism, were expressed with ineffable grace in every attitude and every feature. Clarissa was adored. Her lover was idolatrous. The woods, the dawning day, the starry heavens, witnessed their mutual vows. The grass pressed by her feet, the air she respired, the shade in which she reposed, were consecrated by her presence.

Her mother marked, with pity, the pro-gress of their mutual passion, which she could not forbid, for her own heart was formed for tenderness, nor could she sanction it, seeing no probability of its being crowned with suc-cess. But the happiness of her daughter was her only wish, and moved by her tears, her sighs, and the ardent prayers of her lover, she at length consented to their union. They were

married and they were happy. But alas! a few
days after their marriage a fever seized Clarissa. The distracted husband flew to her father who refused to send her the least assistance. She languished, and her mother and
her husband hung over her in all the bitterness
of anguish. The impossibility of paying a
physician prevented their calling one, till it
was too late, and, ten days after she had become a wife, she expired. I have held this
disconsolate mother to my breast, my tears
have mingled with hers: all the ties that bound
her to the world are severed, and she wishes
only for the moment that will put a period to
her existence, when she fondly hopes she may
be again united to her daughter. To the husband I have never uttered a word. His sorrow
is deep and gloomy. He avoids all conversation, and an attempt to console him would be
an insult on the sacredness of his grief. He
has tasted celestial joys. He has lost the object of his love, and henceforth the earth is for
him a desert.

For the brutal father there is no punishment. His conscience itself inflicts none, for

he expressed not the least regret when inform
ed of the fate of his daughter.

But when the story became known, the
detestation his conduct excited was so violent,
that the friends of Madame C—— have caused her to be separated from him, and obliged
him to allow her a separate maintenance. Unfortunately their interest has been exerted too
late. A few weeks sooner it might have saved
her daughter.

How terrible is the fate of a woman thus
dependent on a man who has lost all sense of
justice, reason, or humanity; who, regardless
of his duties, or the respect he owes society,
leaves his wife to contend with all the pains of
want, and sees his child sink to an untimely
grave, without stretching forth a hand to assist
the one or save the other!

LETTER XIX.

St. Jago de Cuba.

I write continually, my dear friend, though the fate of my letters is very uncertain. If they arrive safe they will prove that I have not forgotten you, and that I suffer no opportunity to pass without informing you that I exist.

I understand that, after our departure from the Cape, the tyranny of the general in chief encreased, and that the inhabitants were daily exposed to new vexations. St. Louis, in particular, was the distinguished object of his hatred. Eternally on guard at the most dangerous posts, it was finally whispered that something, more decidedly bad, was intended him, and he thought it was time to try to escape from the threatening danger. Being informed of a vessel, that was on the point of

sailing, he prevailed on a fisherman to put
him outside of the fort in his boat, and wait
till it came out, the captain not daring to take
him on board in the harbour. On the day
appointed, St. Louis, disguised as a fisherman,
went into the boat, and, working at the oar,
they were soon beyond the fort. The vessel
approached shortly after, and St. Louis, embarking, thought himself out of danger. As
soon as they were in reach of the English ships
they were boarded, plundered and sent to
Barracoa

St. Louis had no trunk, nor any clothes but
what were on him, in which however was concealed gold to a great amount.

A gentleman, who left the Cape the day
after him, informed us of his escape, and of his
having been sent to Barracoa, and also that, as
soon as the general had heard of his departure,
he had sent three barges after the vessel with
orders to seize him, take him back, and, as
soon as he was landed, shoot him without
further ceremony.

The whole town was in the greatest consternation. The barges were well manned and

gained on the vessel, but a light wind spring-
ing up put it soon beyond their reach, and it
was even believed that the officer, who commanded the barges, did not use all possible
diligence to overtake them.

We were rejoiced to hear of the fortunate
escape of St. Louis but felt some anxiety at
his not arriving, when lo! he appeared and
gave us himself an account of his adventures.

He is in raptures with the governor of Barracoa, his charming wife and the good father
Philip, who, hearing that he was the husband
of Clara, shewed him the most friendly attention. He brought us from them letters glowing with affectionate recollection.

He talks of buying a plantation and of
settling here. If he does I shall endeavour to
return to the continent, but poor Clara! she
weeps when I speak of leaving her, and when
I consider the loneliness to which she will be
condemned without me, I have almost heroism
enough to sacrifice my happiness to her com
fort.

Before the arrival of St. Louis we lived in
the house of the gentleman to whose care he

N

had recommended us.   He is a widower, the
most cheerful creature in the world, but he
lives in the times that are past; all his stories
are at least forty years old.   He talks continually of the mystification of Beaumarchais, and
of the magic of Cagliostro.   He told me, with
all the solemnity of truth, that a lady at the
court of France, who was past fifty, bought
from Cagliostro, at a great price, a liquid, a
single drop of which would take off, in appearance, ten years of age.   The lady swallowed
two drops, and went to the opera with her
charms renewed, and her bloom restored to
the freshness of thirty.—At her return she
called her waiting woman, who had been her
nurse and was at least seventy.   She was no-
where to be found, but a little girl came skipping in.   The lady, enquiring who she was,
learned that old Ursula, intending to try the
effect of the drops, had taken too large a dose,
and was skipping about with all the sprightli-
ness of fifteen.

Nothing enrages the old gentleman so
much as to doubt the truth of what he relates,
or even to question its probability.   He assur-

ed me that he knew the lady, and that he witnessed the effect of the drops on herself and
the chambermaid. As I can discover no purpose the invention of such a tale would answer, I listen without reply, and almost suffer
myself to be persuaded of its reality.

Nothing can equal the unpleasantness of
this town : it is built on the declivity of a hill;
the streets are not paved; and the soil, being
of white clay, the reflection is intolerable, and
the heat insupportable. The water is brought
on mules, from a river three miles off, and is
a very expensive article. The women never
walk, except to church, but every evening
they take the air in an open cabriolet, drawn
by mules, in which they exhibit their finery,
and, not unfrequently, regale themselves with
a segar.

Every body smokes, at all times, and in
all places; and from this villanous custom ari-
ses perhaps, the badness of their teeth, which
is universal.

The American consul, who has lived here
many years, says that the people are much
improved since he resided among them. At

his arrival there was not a gown in the place.
They are now generally worn.

This old consul is the greatest beau in the
place. He gives agreeable parties, and makes
love to every body, but I believe with little
success. His very appearance would put all
the loves to flight.

LETTER XX.

St. Jago de Cuba.

The French emigrants begin to seek in their talents some resource from the frightful poverty to which they are reduced, but meet with very little encouragement. The people here are generally poor, and unaccustomed to expensive pleasures. A company of comedians are building a theatre; and some subscription balls have been given, at which the Spanish ladies were quite eclipsed by the French belles, notwithstanding their losses.

Madame D——, of Jeremie, who plays and sings divinely, gave a concert, which was very brilliant.

The French women are certainly charming creatures in society. The cheerfulness with which they bear misfortune, and the industry they employ to procure themselves a

N 2

subsistence, cannot be sufficiently admired. I
know ladies who from their infancy were sur.
rounded by slaves, anticipating their slightest
wishes, now working from the dawn of day
till midnight to support themselves and their
families. Nor do they even complain, nor
vaunt their industry, nor think it surprising
that they possess it. Their neatness is worthy of admiration, and their taste gives to their
attire an air of fashion which the expensive,
but ill-chosen, ornaments of the Spanish ladies cannot attain. With one young lady I
am particularly acquainted whose goodness
cannot be sufficiently admired. Ah! Eliza,
how shall I describe thy sweetness, thy fidelity, thy devotion to a suffering friend. Why
am I not rich that I could place thee in a situation where thy virtues might be known, thy
talents honoured. Alas! I never so deeply regret my own want of power as when reflect-
ing that I am unable to be useful to you.

This amiable girl was left by her parents,
who went to Charleston at the beginning of
the revolution, to the care of an aunt, who was
very rich, and without children. At the eva-

cuation of Port-au-Prince, that lady embarked for this place. Her husband died on the
passage; and they were robbed of every thing
they possessed by an English privateer. The
father of Eliza wrote for them to join him in
Carolina; but the ill health of madame L——
would not suffer her to undertake the voyage,
and Eliza will not hear of leaving her, but
works day and night to procure for her aunt
the comforts her situation requires. She is
young, beautiful and accomplished. She
wastes her bloom over the midnight lamp,
and sacrifices her health and her rest to soothe
the sufferings of her infirm relation. Her patience and mildness are angelic. Where will
such virtues meet their reward? Certainly not
in this country; and she is held here by the
ties of gratitude and affection which, to a heart
like hers, are indissoluble.

In the misfortunes of my French friends,
I see clearly exemplified the advantages of a
good education. Every talent, even if possessed in a slight degree of perfection, may be
a resource in a reverse of fortune; and, though
I liked not entirely their manner, whilst sur-

rounded by the festivity and splendour of the
Cape, I now confess that they excite my warmest admiration.   They bear adversity with
cheerfulness, and resist it with fortitude.   In
the same circumstances I fear I should be inferior to them in both.   But in this country,
slowly emerging from a state of barbarism,
what encouragment can be found for industry
or talents?   The right of commerce was purchased by the Catalonians, who alone exercise
it, and agriculture is destroyed in consequence
of the restraints imposed on it by the government.   The people are poor, and therefore
cannot possess talents whose acquisition is beyond their reach; but they are temperate,
even to a proverb, and so hospitable that the
poorest among them always find something to
offer to a stranger.   At the same time they are
said to be false, treacherous, and revengeful,
to the highest degree.   Certainly there are
here no traces of that magnanimous spirit,
which once animated the Spanish cavalier, who
was considered by the whole world as a model of constancy, tenderness and heroism.

They feel for the distressed, because they are poor; and are hospitable because they know want. In every other respect this is a degenerate race, possessing none of the qualities of the Spaniards of old except jealousy, which is often the cause of tragical events.

A young gentleman of this place fell in love with a beautiful girl who rejected him because she was secretly attached to another. Her lover was absent; and she feared to avow her passion lest his rival might use some means to destroy him, for she knew he was cruel and vindictive; but her lover returning, she declared her attachment, and declined receiving the visits of him who had pretended to her hand. A few evenings previous to that fixed on for her marriage, she was returning from church with her mother, when at the door of her house a man, wrapped in a large cloak, seized her arm, and plunging a dagger in her breast, fled, leaving her lifeless on the ground. The cries of her affrighted mother brought people to her assistance, but the blow was directed by a secure hand; she breathed no more. Every body was convinced that the

perpetrator of this abominable act was her rejected lover; but, as no proofs existed, the
law could not interfere. Shortly after he was
found dead in the street; and probably it was
the hand of him he had driven to despair, that
inflicted the punishment due to his crime.

Nothing is more common than such events.
They excite little attention, and are seldom
enquired into. How different is this from the
peaceful security of the country in which I
first drew breath, and to which I so ardently,
but I fear hopelessly, desire to return.

LETTER XX

—

St. Jago de Cuba.

General Rochambeau, after having made a shameful capitulation with the negroes, has evacuated the Cape. He presented his superb horses to Dessalines, and then embarked with his suite, and all the inhabitants who chose to follow him, intending to fight his way through the British ships. They were, however, soon overpowered and taken. The English admiral would not admit the general in chief into his presence. He has been sent to Jamaica, from whence he will be transported to England.

Many of the inhabitants of the Cape have arrived here, after having lost every thing they possessed. Numbers have remained. After the articles of capitulation were signed three days were allowed for the evacuation, during

which the negroes entered the town, and were
so civil and treated the inhabitants with so
much kindness and respect, that many who
had embarked their effects, allured by the
prospect of making a fortune rapidly, paid
great sums to have them relanded, supposir g
they would be protected as they had been in
the time of Toussaint. But in less than a
week they found that they had flattered themselves with false hopes. A proclamation was
issued by Dessalines, in which every white
man was declared an enemy of the *indigenes*,
as they call themselves, and their colour alone
deemed sufficient to make them hated and to
devote them to destruction. The author of
this eloquent production, a white man, became himself the first sacrifice.

The destined victims were assembled in a
public square, where they were slaughtered
by the negroes with the most unexampled
cruelty. One brave man, who had often distinguished himself in the defence of the Cape,
and who had been weak enough to stay in it,
seized with desperate fury the sword of one of
the negroes, and killing several, at length fell,

overpowered by numbers. A few were preserved from this day's massacre by their slaves.
Some were concealed by the American merchants, though it was very dangerous to venture on such benevolent actions. One vessel
was searched, and several inhabitants being
found on board, they were taken and hanged.
The mate of the vessel, though an American,
shared their fate. The captain saved himself
by declaring that he was ignorant of their being on board. Major B——, whom I have so
often mentioned, had also the folly to stay.
One of his slaves concealed him on the day of
the massacre, and, shut up in a hogshead, he
was put on board an American vessel. After
many perilous adventures he has arrived here,
and relates scenes which cannot be thought of
without horror.

The women have not yet been killed; but
they are exposed to every kind of insult, are
driven from their houses, imprisoned, sent to
work on the public roads; in fine, nothing can
be imagined more dreadful than their situation.

Two amiable girls, whom I knew, hung

o

to the neck of their father when the negroes seized him. They wept and entreated these monsters to spare him; but he was torn rudely from their arms. The youngest, attempting to follow him, received a blow on the head with a musquet which laid her lifeless on the ground. The eldest, frantic with terror, clung to her father, when a ruthless negro pierced her with his bayonet, and she fell dead at his feet. The hapless father gave thanks to God that his unfortunate children had perished before him, and had not been exposed to lingering sufferings and a more dreadful fate.

Some ladies have found protectors in the American merchants, who conceal them in their stores. Some have been saved by the British officers; but the greatest number have been driven into the streets, and many are forced to carry on their heads baskets of cannon balls from the arsenal to the fosset, a distance of at least three miles.

I enquired after a most accomplished and exemplary woman, who with three beautiful daughters remained at the Cape after the eva

cuation, and I have wept at the story of their
sufferings till I am unable to relate them.

What could have induced these infatuated
people to confide in the promises of the negroes? Yet to what will not people submit to
avoid the horrors of poverty, or allured by the
hope of making a rapid fortune.

During the reign of Toussaint the white
inhabitants had been generally respected, and
many of them, engaging in commerce, had
accumulated money which they sent to the
United States, where they are now living at
their ease. Even at the arrival of the French
fleet, the lives of the people, except in a few
solitary instances, had been spared. These
considerations had without doubt great weight,
but alas! how soon were their hopes blasted,
and how dearly have they paid for their credu-
lity. Yet even these monsters, thirsting after
blood, and unsated with carnage, preserved
from among the devoted victims those whose
talents could be useful to themselves. A
printer and several artists have been suffered
to live, but are closely guarded, and warned
that their lives will be the forfeit of the first

attempt to escape. With the sword suspended over their heads they still cherish perhaps a secret hope of eluding the vigilance of their savage masters.

LETTER XXII.

—

St. Jago de Cuba.

Madame G——, a native of the Gonaives, having lost her husband at the beginning of the revolution, left St. Domingo, and sought a retreat from the horrors that ravaged that devoted island in the peaceful obscurity of Barracoa. Three infant daughters cheered her solitude; and she found in cultivating their minds a never failing source of delight. Some faithful slaves who had followed her, supplied by their industry her wants. The beauty of her person, the elegance of her manners, and the propriety of her conduct, rendered her the admiration of all who beheld her, whilst her benevolence, which shared with the poor the scanty pittance she possessed, made her the idol of those whose wants she relieved. Thus she lived, contented, if not happy, till the ar-

o 2

rival of the French army at St. Domingo re-
called its inhabitants to their deserted homes.

Madame G——, lured by the hope of re-
instating her children in their paternal inheritance, left Barracoa, followed by the blessings
and regret of all to whom she was known.
On arriving at the Cape she found a heap of
ashes, and shuddered with horror at the dreary
aspect of her native country. But she viewed
her children, recollected that on her exertions
they depended, and determined to sacrifice
every thought of comfort to their advance-
ment. Some houses she owned in the Cape,
upon being rebuilt, promised to yield her a
handsome revenue; and she passed in anxious
expectation the time during which the army
kept possession of the Cape. At length the
moment of the evacuation arrived, and the
wretched Creoles were again reduced to the
dreadful alternative of perishing with want in
foreign countries, or of becoming victims to
the rage of the exasperated negroes in their
own. Whilst Madame G—— hesitated, she
received a letter from one of the black chiefs,
who had been a slave to her mother. He ad-

vised her not to think of leaving the country; assured her that it was the intention of Dessalines to protect all the white inhabitants who put confidence in him, and that herself and her children would be particularly respected. The dread of poverty in a strange country with three girls, the eldest of whom was only fifteen, induced her to stay. Many others, with less reason to expect protection, followed her example.

When the time allowed for the evacuation had expired, the negroes entered as masters. During the first days reigned a deceitful calm which was followed by a dreadful storm.

The proclamation of Dessalines, mentioned in my last letter was published. Armed negroes entered the houses and drove the inhabitants into the streets. The men were led to prison, the women were loaded with chains. The unfortunate madame G——, chained to her eldest daughter, and the two youngest chained together, thus toiled, exposed to the sun, from earliest dawn to setting day, followed by negroes who, on the least appearance of faintness, drove them forward with whips. A fortnight later the general massacre took place, but the four hopeless beings of whom I particularly write, were not led to the field of slaughter. They were kept closely guarded, without knowing for what fate they were reserved, expecting every moment to hear their final sentence. They were sitting one day in mournful silence, when the door of their prison opened, and the chief, whose letter had induced them to stay, appeared. He saluted madame G—— with great familiarity, told her it was to his orders she owed her life, and said he would continue his friendship and protection if she would give him her eldest daughter in marriage. The wretched mother caught the terrified Adelaide, who sunk fainting into her arms. The menacing looks of the negro became more horrible. He advanced to seize the trembling girl. Touch her not, cried the frantic mother; death will be preferable to such protection. Turning coldly from her he said, You shall have your choice. A few minutes after a guard seized the mother and the two youngest daughters and carried them out, leaving the eldest insensible on the floor.

They were borne to a gallows which had been erected before their prison, and immediately hanged. Adelaide was then carried to the house of the treacherous chief, who informed her of the fate of her mother, and asked her if she would consent to become his wife? ah! no, she replied, let me follow my mother. A fate more dreadful awaited her. The monster gave her to his guard, who hung her by the throat on an iron hook in the market place, where the lovely, innocent, unfortunate victim slowly expired.

LETTER XXIII.

—

St. Jago de Cuba.

I finished my last letter abruptly, my dear friend, but a good opportunity offered of sending it, and the story of madame G—— had so affected me that I could think of nothing else.

St. Louis is determined to buy a plantation here, and establish himself on it till he can return to St. Domingo. His old disease has seized him with fresh violence, and he intends to carry his wife beyond the reach of men. He is jealous of an interesting Spaniard who has lately been very assiduous towards my sister; and who is, I believe, much more dangerous than the redoubted general Rochambeau. His person is perfectly elegant; his face beautiful; his large black eyes seem to speak every emotion of his soul, but I be-

lieve they express only what he pleases. Clara
listens to him, and looks at him as if she was
fully sensible of his advantages, and frequently
holds long conversations with him in his own
language, which, if gestures deceive not, are
on no uninteresting subject. But I hope, and
would venture to assert, that she will never,
to escape from the domestic ills she suffers,
put her happiness in the power of a Spaniard.
She is violent in her attachments, and preci-
pitate in her movements, but she cannot, will
not, be capable of committing such an unpar-
donable act of folly. All idea of her going to
the continent is abandoned; and when I only
breathe a hint of leaving her, she betrays such
agony that I yield and promise to stay; yet I
render her little service, and destroy myself,
being wearied of this place, which has no
charm after the gloss of novelty is gone, and
that has been long since worn off.

A company of French comedians had built
a theatre here, and obtained permission from
the governor to perform. They played with
eclat, and always to crowded houses. The
Spaniards were delighted. The decorations,

the scenery, above all the representation of the
sea, appeared to them the effect of magic. But
the charm was suddenly dissolved by an order
from the bishop to close the theatre, saying,
that it tended to corrupt the morals of the inhabitants. Nothing can be more ridiculous,
for the inhabitants of this island have long
since reached the last degree of corruption;
devoted to every species of vice, guilty of
every crime, and polluted by the continued
practice of every species of debauchery. But
it is supposed the order was issued to vex the
governor, with whom the bishop is at variance,
and the orders of the latter are indisputable.
It is impossible for him not to know that even
the vices of the French lose much of their de-
formity by the refinement that accompanies
them, whilst those of his countrymen are
gross, disgusting, and monstrously flagrant.
Gaming is their ruling passion; from morning
till night, from night till morning, the men are
at the gaming table. They all wear daggers,
and a night very seldom passes without being
marked by an assassination, of which no notice is taken. The women have recourse to

P

intrigue, sipping chocolate, or reciting prayers on their rosaries. The custom is to dine at twelve, then to sleep till three, and this is the hour favourable to amorous adventures. Whilst the mother, the husband or the guardian sleeps, the lover silently approaches the window of his mistress, and in smothered accents breathes his passion. It is not at all uncommon to see priests so employed; nor are there more dangerous enemies to female virtue, or domestic tranquillity, than these pretended servants of the Lord.

I was at first shocked beyond measure, at their licentiousness, for I had been taught to consider priests as immaculate beings; but when I reflect that they are men, and doomed to an unnatural condition, I pardon their aberrations, and abhor only their filth, which is abominable. Consider how agreeable a monk must be in this hot country, clothed in woollen, without a shirt, without stockings, and his legs so dirty that their colour cannot be distinguished, to which is added a long beard; and yet these creatures are favourites with women of all ranks and all descriptions.

There are many religious orders here, among which the Franciscan friars are the richest, and they are also the most irregular in their conduct. They had begun, a number of years since, to build a church, which they were obliged to discontinue for want of funds. Shortly after our arrival here the wife of a very rich merchant fell dangerously ill. When her life was despaired of by the physicians, she made a vow to St. Francis, that if she recovered, she would finish his church. The saint, it seems, was propitious, for she was restored to health, and her husband instantly performed the promise of his wife, which has cost him a hundred and fifty thousand dollars. The church was consecrated last week, with great pomp and due solemnity. The lady, who is certainly very beautiful, assisted at the ceremony, covered with diamonds, and displaying in her dress almost regal splendour. She kneeled on the steps of the great altar, and more than shared the adoration offered to the saint by the admiring multitude.

Half the money expended in this pious work would have raised thousands of the in-

habitants of this place, who are in the greatest
want, to comparative ease.   But it would not
if thus employed, have had such an effect on
the minds of the people; nor would the lady
have had any hope of becoming herself a saint,
an honour to which she aspires, and which she
may perhaps attain.

LETTER XXIV.

—

St. Jago de Cuba.

Clara and her husband are separated for
ever! St. Louis is frantic, and I am distressed
beyond measure. My heart is torn with anxiety
for her fate, and I shall know no tranquillity
till I hear that she is at least content. Being
acquainted with many of the circumstances
which led to this event, I pity and pardon her.
As for the world, its sentence is already pro-
nounced, and she will be condemned by those
who possess not a thousandth part of her virtues. Her husband spares neither pains nor
expense in searching after her retreat; but,
though I am absolutely ignorant of it, I believe she is beyond his reach. His house is
so disagreeable to me, since she left it, and
the wry faces made by all our friends, seem-
ing to involve me in the scandal occasioned by

P 2

her elopement, excite such unpleasant sensations that it will be impossible for me to remain here. Therefore I shall leave this place
immediately with a lady who is going to establish herself in Jamaica. I have always desired to see that island, and there I intend to
stay till I have some positive information of
Clara. If she is gone to the continent I shall
follow her immediately; if she is in Cuba my
friendship, my presence will console her, and
they shall not be wanting. One of my friends,
a man of intelligence and discretion, has promised to find her, if possible, and has promised
also not to betray her, for she must never be
restored to the power of her husband. Far
from being an advocate for the breach of vows
so sacred as those which bound her to St.
Louis, I have always expressed with unqualified warmth, my disapprobation of the levity
of many women who had abandoned their husbands. But there are circumstances which
palliate error. Many of those which led to
Clara's elopement plead for her; but if she
has sought protection with another, if she will

not accompany me, my heart renounces her, and she will no longer have a sister.

We sail in three days. St. Louis makes no objection to my going, and I leave Cuba without regret, for in it I have never been happy. Write to me at Kingston. Never was the assurance of your friendship more necessary to my heart than at this moment.

LETTER XXV.

—

Kingston, Jamaica.

We arrived at Kingston after a passage of
twenty-four hours.   On entering the harbour
our little vessel, as it passed near the admiral's
ship, appeared like an ant at the foot of a
mountain.   Nothing is more delightful than
the bustle and continual movement that strikes
the eye on entering this port.   Innumerable
boats are continually plying round the vessels,
offering for sale all the fruits of the season.   I
like the town.   There is an air of neatness in
the houses which I have no where seen since
I left my own country; but the streets are de-
testable; none of them are paved, and at every
step you sink ankle deep in sand.

I have found numbers of my French friends
here, and among others madame M——, who
was more than gallant at the Cape, and who at

St. Jago appeared not insensible to the pleasure of being loved. She left her sister in a
fit of jealousy and went to Jamaica, hoping to
captivate some Englishman, or at least to rival
him in his attachment to roast beef and Ma-
deira. But it seems she has been disappointed,
no lover having yet offered his homage to her
robust attractions. She accuses them of wanting taste, and hates the place and all who in-
habit it.

I have also met here my little friend Coralie, whose adventures since I parted with her
at the Cape, have been distressing and romantic.

Her mother and herself had been persuaded to remain at the Cape, after the evacuation, by a brother on whom they entirely depended, and who, seduced by the hope of
making a fortune, staid and shared the melancholy fate of the white inhabitants of that
place. Coralie and her sister were concealed
by an American merchant in his store, among
sacks of coffee and boxes of sugar. Their
mother had been led, with the rest of the women, to the field of slaughter.

The benevolent man who concealed these unfortunate girls at the risk of his life, after some weeks had elapsed, and the vigilance of the negroes a little relaxed, entreated the captain of an English frigate to receive them on board his vessel, to which he readily agreed. Disguised in sailors' clothes, and carrying baskets of provisions on their heads, they followed the captain to the sea side. As they approached the guard placed on the wharf to examine all that embarked, they trembled, and involuntarily drew back. But their brave protector told them that it was too late to recede, and that he would defend them with his life. As the English were on the best terms with the negroes, the supposed boys were suffered to pass. On entering the ship the captain congratulated them on their escape, and Coralie, overpowered by a variety of sensations, fainted in the arms of her generous protector.

A few days after, they sailed for Jamaica. On entering Port Royal, the frigate was driven against a small vessel, and so damaged it, that it appeared to be sinking. The boat was instantly hoisted out, and the captain of the

frigate went himself to the assistance of the
sufferers. The passengers and crew jumped
into the boat, and were making off, when the
screams of a female were heard from below,
and it was recollected that there was a sick
lady in the cabin. The English captain descended, brought her up in his arms, and put
her in the boat. Then, saying that the vessel
was not so much injured as they imagined,
ordered some of his people to assist him in
saving many things that lay at hand. Four
sailors jumped on board, and followed their
commander to the cabin, where they had
scarcely descended, when the vessel suddenly
filled and sunk. They were irrecoverably
lost.

Coralie, standing on the deck of the frigate, beheld this catastrophe, saw perish the
man to whom she owed her life, and whose
subsequent kindness had won her heart.

The lady found in the sinking vessel was
her mother, who had escaped almost miracu-
lously from the Cape, fully persuaded that her
daughters existed no longer. The joy of their
meeting was damped by the melancholy fate

of their deliverer, which has been universally
lamented.

The scenes of barbarity, which these girls
have witnessed at the Cape, are almost incredible. The horror, however, which I felt on
hearing an account of them, has been relieved
by the relation of some more honourable to
human nature. In the first days of the massacre; when the negroes ran through the town
killing all the white men they encountered, a
Frenchman was dragged from the place of his
concealment by a ruthless mulatto, who, drawing his sabre, bade him prepare to die. The
trembling victim raised a supplicating look,
and the murderer, letting fall his uplifted arm,
asked if he had any money. He replied, that
he had none ; but that if he would conduct
him to the house of an American merchant,
he might probably procure any sum he might
require. The mulatto consented, and when
they entered the house, the Frenchman with
all the energy of one pleading for his life, entreated the American to lend him a consider-
able sum. The gentleman he addressed was
too well acquainted with the villainy of the

Q

negroes to trust to their word. He told the mulatto, that he would give the two thousand dollars demanded, but not till the Frenchman was embarked in a vessel which was going to sail in a few days for Philadelphia, and entirely out of danger. The mulatto refused. The unfortunate Frenchman wept, and the American kept firm. While they were disputing, a girl of colour, who lived with the American, entered, and having learned the story, employed all her eloquence to make the mulatto relent. She sunk at his feet, and pressed his hands which were reeking with blood. Dear brother, she said, spare for my sake this unfortunate man. He never injured you; nor will you derive any advantage from his death, and by saving him, you will acquire the sum you demand, and a claim to his gratitude. She was beautiful; she wept, and beauty in tears has seldom been resisted. Yet this unrelenting savage did resist; and swore, with bitter oaths to pursue all white men with unremitting fury. The girl, however, hung to him, repeated her solicitations, and offered him, in addition to the sum proposed, all her trinkets, which were of considerable value.

The mulatto, enraged, asked if the Frenchman was any thing to her? Nothing, she replied; I never saw him before; but to save the life of an innocent person how trifling would appear the sacrifice I offer. She continued her entreaties in the most caressing tone, which for some time had no effect, when softening all at once, he said, I will not deprive you of your trinkets, nor is it for the sum proposed that I relent, but for you alone, for to you I feel that I can refuse nothing. He shall be concealed, and guarded by myself till the moment of embarking; but, when he is out of danger, you must listen to me in your turn.

She heard him with horror; but, dissembling, said there would be always time enough to think of those concerns. She was then too much occupied by the object before her.

The American, who stood by and heard this proposal, made to one to whom he was extremely attached, felt disposed to knock the fellow down, but the piteous aspect of the al-

most expiring Frenchman withheld his hand.
He gave the mulatto a note for the money he
had demanded, on the conditions before mentioned, and the Frenchman was faithfully concealed till the vessel was ready to sail, and then
embarked.

When he was gone, the mulatto called on
the girl, and offering her the note, told her
her that he had accepted it as a matter of form,
but that he now gave it to her; and reminded
her of the promise she had made to listen to
his wishes.   Her lover entering at that moment told him that the vessel was then out of
the harbour, and that his money was ready.
He took it, and thus being in the power of the
American gentleman, who had great weight
with Dessalines, he probably thought it best
to relinquish his projects on the charming Zu-
line, for she heard of him no more.

The same girl was the means of saving
many others, and the accounts I have heard
of her kindness and generosity oblige me to
think of her with unqualified admiration.

LETTER XXVI.

———

Kingston, Jamaica.

I pass my time agreeably enough here,
though I am obliged to stay in a boarding
house till madame L—— can be fixed in her
own. A few days ago a Spanish sloop of war
was captured by a British frigate, and brought
into Jamaica. The officers were suffered to
land, and came to lodge in the house where I
stay. When called to dinner I was surprized
at finding myself among a group of strangers.
As the mistress of the house never dines at
table, and madame L—— was abroad, I would
have retreated, but curiosity prompted me to
remain.

The Spanish captain is an elderly man of
most respectable appearance. All the rest are
young, full of spirits, and two of them remarkably beautiful. Taking it for granted that I

Q 2

was French, and not imagining I could understand their language, as soon as they were
seated at table they indulged very freely in
their remarks on myself. One said I was not
pretty; another, that I was interesting; another, that I resembled somebody he had seen
before; and one elegant young man, who sat
next me, having brushed his arm against mine
made in Spanish an apology, which I appeared not to understand. He then asked me if
I spoke English? I shook my head ; and he
observed to his companions, that he had never
so much regretted his ignorance of the French.
They laughed ; and he continued lamenting
the impossibility of making himself understood. After dinner I withdrew, and having
been engaged by Coralie to pass the evening
at her house, I forgot the strangers, and
thought of them no more till the next morning at breakfast, where they were all assembled, and where madame L—— related to me
an adventure she had met with the day before.
She spoke English, and as I was answering
her my eyes met those of the young officer,
and his look covered me with confusion. Ah!

he said, you speak English, and were cruel
enough to refuse holding converse with a
stranger and a prisoner. I speak so little, I
replied. No, no, he cried, your accent is not
foreign; I could almost swear that it is your
native language. He looked at the others
with an ir of triumph; and the one who had
said I was not pretty, observed, that he was
glad I did not speak Spanish; but I understand it perfectly, I answered in the same language.

He looked petrified; and the old captain
was delighted. He made many inquiries after
his friends at Cuba, with all of whom I was
acquainted. The young officer who speaks
English, is by birth an Irishman. He entered the Spanish service at the age of fifteen;
had been several years at Lima; had returned to Europe, and was on his way to Vera
Cruz when they were taken by the English.
With him my heart claimed kindred, for in
every Irishman I fancy I behold a brother and
a friend. His manners are elegant and interesting beyond expression. There is an appearance of sadness in his face, which height-

ens the interest his fine form creates; and if I
had an unoccupied heart, and he a heart to offer, I believe we should soon forget that he is
a prisoner and I a stranger!

I have learned from him, that on his arrival at Lima, he was lodged in the house of a
gentleman who had a beautiful daughter. She
was a widow, though very young. The se-
clusion in which the ladies of this county live
rendred such a companion as Don Carlos
doubly dangerous, and the beauty and sweetness of Donna Angelina, made an indelible
impression on his heart. Their mutual passion
was soon acknowledged; but obstacles, which
appeared' insurmountable, seemed to deprive
them even of hope.

Angelina had inherited the immense fortune left by her husband, on condition of re-
maining a widow. Her father was very rich,
but avarice was his ruling passion. He had
sacrificed his only child at the age of thirteen
to an old man, merely because he was wealthy, and there was no reason to expect that he
would suffer her to abandon the fortune she
had so dearly acquired, and marry a man who

had no inheritance but his sword. Though
these considerations cast a cloud over their
mutual prospects, they still cherished their
mutual affection, and hoped that some fortunate event would at length render them happy.
The father of Angelina never suspected the
situation of his daughter's heart, and her intercourse with Don Carlos was without restraint. Delightful moments of visionary happiness how quickly ye passed; delivering in
your flight two victims to the gripe of despair!

A new viceroy arrived from Spain and
Angelina was obliged to appear at a ball given
to celebrate his entry into Lima.

She danced with Don Carlos, and her
beauty, eclipsing all other beauty, attracted
universal notice, but particularly that of the
viceroy, who went the next day to offer at her
feet the homage of his adoration. She received him coldly, but the father was transported with joy, and when, a few days after,
the viceroy demanded her hand, without hesitation favoured his suit. Angelina declined,
and acquainted him with the conditions on
which she inherited her husband's wealth, and

her resolution to remain a widow. He told her that his own fortune was more than sufficient to replace that he wished her to sacrifice, but her evident aversion raised a suspicion of other reasons than those she avowed, and his jealous watchfulness soon discovered her attachment to Don Carlos. He informed her father of his discovery, who, furious at seeing his hopes of aggrandizing his family thwarted by a boy, forbad all intercourse between them.

The means employed by the viceroy to separate them were still more effectual. A vessel was on the point of sailing for Spain, and Don Carlos received orders to embark instantly to bear dispatches of importance to the court. Resistance would have been vain. He sailed without being permitted to see the object he had so long adored.

When he arrived in Spain, he learned that his rival had taken every precaution to prevent his return to Lima. Fortunately he knew the heart of his Angelina, and felt assured that the hopes of that detested rival would never be crowned with success; nor was he disappointed.

She had been deprived by her father and the viceroy of the man she loved, but their power extended no farther. There was an asylum to which she could retreat from their tyranny; that asylum was a convent. She entered one, took the vows, and gave her immense fortune to the society of which she became a member.

On the eve of entering the convent she wrote to Don Carlos, informing him of her intention; of the impossibility of preserving herself for him, and her determination never to belong to another. He received this letter the day on which he sailed for Vera Cruz, and I believe, does not regret being a prisoner, since he has found in the place of his captivity a kind being who listens to his tale of sorrows and seeks to pour the balm of consolation into his wounded heart.

He amuses me continually with his stories of Lima; describing the splendour of its palaces, the magnificence of its churches, filled with golden saints and silver angels, and the beautiful women with which it abounds. He tells me there can be nothing more fascinating

than their manners; nor more singular and
picturesque than their dress, which consists of
a petticoat, reaching no lower than the knee,
and a veil that covers the head and waist, but
through which a pretty face is often shewn in
a most bewitching manner. At the same time
I perceive that he talks on every subject with
reluctance, except on that nearest his heart;
and when speaking of this, he seems animated by all the energy of despair.

I have heard of Clara by a person just arrived from Cuba, and have written to her.
My heart is torn with anxiety for her fate, and
will remain a stranger to repose till I receive
more satisfactory intelligence. I fear she was
not born to be at ease. She lives continually
in an ideal world. Her enthusiastic imagination filled with forms which it creates at pleasure, cherishes a romantic hope of visionary
happiness which never can be realized.

Yet with all my fine sentiments of correct-
ness and propriety, and the duty of content and
resignation, my heart refuses to condemn her
for having left her husband. Never was there
any thing more directly opposite than the soul

of Clara, and that of the man to whom she was
united. Their tempers, their dispositions, were
absolutely incompatible. And should I abandon this poor girl to misfortune? should I
leave her to perish among strangers? ah! no,
she is twined round my heart, and I love her
with more than a sister's affection.   As soon
as I hear from her again, you shall be informed of my intentions.   If I can induce her to
return with me to Philadelphia, in rejoining
you I shall think myself no longer unhappy.

LETTER XXVII.

———

To Clara.

Kingston, Jamaica.

I have received the message, sent me by
Anselmo, my dear Clara, and my joy at hearing of your welfare, made me forget for a moment, the many causes you have given me of
complaint. Yet what more have I learned
than that you exist? of all that concerns you
I remain ignorant. Unkind Clara! thus you
repay my friendship! thus console me for all
the solicitude I have felt for you! To have
staid with St. Louis, after you left him, was
not possible, for he did not conceal his suspi-
cions of my having been in your secret, nor
could I find in Cuba an eligible retreat; for
all my friends were his, and all disposed to
condemn you. I accepted therefore, with plea-

sure, the offer made by Madame L——, to take me with her to Jamaica.

Write to me, my dear sister, immediately. Tell me every thing. Does not your heart require the affectionate sympathy it has been accustomed to receive from mine? Can you live without me?—without me who have followed you, and love you with an affection so tender? Dearest Clara, speak, and I will fly to you! Means shall be found to return to Philadelphia, where, in peaceful obscurity we may live, free from the cares which have tormented you, and filled myself with anxiety.

Anselmo will be careful of your letter. Write fully, and remember that you are writing to more than a sister; to a friend, who loves you, who adores your virtues, and who pardons, while she weeps, your faults!

LETTER XXVIII.

To Mary ——.

Bayam, 20 leagues from St. Jago.

I know your heart, my dear Mary! On the affection which glows for me in that heart, I have counted for the pardon of my errors, and your letter convinces me that I have not been deceived. You know for you witnessed, my domestic infelicity ; yet, how many of my pains did I not conceal, to spare you the anguish of lamenting sorrows which you could not alleviate !

St. Louis, after his arrival at St. Jago, had connected himself with a company of gamesters, and with them passed all his time.—— Often returning at a late hour from the gaming table, he has treated me with the most brutal violence,—this you never knew ; nor

many things which passed in the loneliness of
my chamber, where, wholly in his power, I
could only oppose to his brutality my tears and
my sighs.   To his intolerable and groundless
jealousy at Cape Francois you were no stranger : it embittered my days.   Since our arrival in this island it increased.   In every man
that approached me he saw a rival! and the
more amiable the object, the more terrible
were his apprehensions.

He became acquainted, at some of the
haunts of gaming, with Don Alonzo de P——
and brought him to our house, but, when his
visits had been repeated two or three times,
all the tortures of jealousy were awakened in
the breast of St. Louis.

If I received this young stranger with pleasure, it was because I found him interesting.
If I avoided him it was an acknowledgement
of his power!

He had insisted on my learning the Spanish
language, yet if I spoke in that language it was
to express sentiments I sought to conceal from
him.   How often, in the bitterness of anguish,
have I thought that the direst poverty would

be preferable to the ease I had purchased at
the expence of my peace! but alas! the colour of my fate was fixed,—I was united to
St. Louis by bonds which I had been taught
to consider sacred, and, though my heart shuddered at the life-long tie, yet I always recoiled
with horror from the idea of breaking it.—
That tie however is broken; those bonds are
dissolved! and there is no fate so dreadful to
which I would not submit, rather than have
them renewed.

Believe me when I assure you that my
flight was not premeditated It is true, the eloquent eyes of Don Alonzo often spoke vo-
lumes, but I never appeared to understand
their language, nor did a look of encouragement ever escape me. For some days previous to my elopement the ill humour of St.
Louis had been intolerable. My wearied soul
sunk beneath the torments I endured and death
would have been preferable to such a state of
existence. The night before I left him he came
home in a transport of fury, dragged me from
mv bed, said it was his intention to destroy me,
and swore that he would render me horrible

by rubbing aqua-fortis in my face. This last menace deprived me of the power of utterance; to kill me would have been a trifling evil, but to live disfigured, perhaps blind, was an insufferable idea and roused me to madness. I passed the night in speechless agony. The only thought I dwelt on was, how to escape from this monster, and, at break of day, I was still sitting, as if rendered motionless by his threats. From this stupor I was roused by his caresses, or rather by his brutal approaches, for he always finds my person provoking, and often, whilst pouring on my head abuse which would seem dictated by the most violent hatred, he has sought in my arms gratifications which should be solicited with affection, and granted to love alone.

You must recollect my unusual sadness that day; for well do I remember the kind efforts you made to divert me.

I awaited the approach of night with gloomy impatience, determined that the dawn of day should not find me beneath that hated roof. When I left you in the evening it was with difficulty I restrained my tears. My heart was breaking at the idea of being separated from you, if not forever at least for a consider-able time, and the thought of the pain my flight would occasion you almost determined me to relinquish it.

But St. Louis was in my chamber, and his presence dispelled every idea, except that of avoiding it forever. After seeing me undress-ed, he left me, as usual, to pass the greatest part of the night abroad. His vigilant guard, the faithful Madelaine, lay down near the door of my apartment, and I, taking a book, appeared to read. At eleven o'clock I knew by her breathing that she was asleep.

Taking off my shoes, I passed her softly— opened the door that leads into the garden, and was instantly in the street.

The moments were precious, for I had the whole town to pass, in order to gain the road to *Cobre*, where I intended to request an asy-lum of Madame V——.

I flew with the rapidity of lightning, nor stopped to breathe till I had passed the town. Beginning to ascend the mountain, I paused, and leaning against a tree, reflected for a mo-

ment on the singularity of my situation.—
Alone, at midnight, on the road to an obscure
village, whose inhabitants are regarded as little better than a horde of banditti!—Flying
from a husband, whose pursuit I dreaded more
than death; leaving behind me a sister, for
whom my heart bled, but whom I could never think of involving in my precarious fate!

The night was calm. The town, which
lies at the foot of the mountain, was buried
in profound repose. The moon-beams glit-
tered on the waves that were rolling in the
bay, and shed their silvery lustre on the moving branches of the palm trees. The silence
was broken by the melodious voice of a bird,
who sings only at this hour, and whose notes
are said to be sweeter than those of the European nightingale. As I ascended the mountain, the air became purer. Every tree in this
delightful region is aromatic; every breeze
wafts prefumes! I had six miles to walk, and
wished to reach the village before day, yet I
could not avoid frequently stopping to enjoy
the delightful calm that reigned around me!

I knew that, as soon as I was missed, the

town would be diligently searched for me, but of the retreat I had chosen St. Louis could have no idea, for he was totally unacquainted with the residence of Madame V———. To this lady I had rendered some essential services at the Cape, which gave me a claim on her friendship. She left that place before us, and on her arrival here, bought a little plantation in. *Cobre*, where she lives in the greatest retirement. I had heard of her by accident, and thought it the surest retreat I could find. As the day broke I perceived the straggling huts which compose this village, and, approaching the most comfortable one of the group, found to my great satisfaction, that it was inhabited by the lady I sought. She had just risen, and was opening the door as I drew near it. Her surprise at seeing me was so great, that she doubted for a moment the evidence of her senses; but, seizing my hand, she led me to her chamber, where, pressed in her arms, I felt that I had found a friend, and the tears that flowed on her bosom were proofs of my gratefulness.

I began to explain to her my situation. "I

know it all!" she cried, "you have escaped
from your husband. My predictions are ve-
rified, though a little later than I expected.—
But where" continued she, "is your sister?"
I replied that my flight had not been premeditated, and that you had not been apprised of
it. There was no necessity for giving her a
reason for having left my husband. She had
always been at a loss to find one for my staying with him so long. The next consideration was my toilette. I was bare-headed, without stockings:—my shoes were torn to pieces
by the ruggedness of the road, and I had no
other covering than a thin muslin morning
gown. The kind friend, who received me,
supplied me with clothes, and checked her eagerness to learn the particulars of my story till
I had taken the repose I so much required.

Towards evening she seated herself by my
bedside, and I related to her all that I had suffered since she left me at the Cape.

But when I spoke of the threat which had
determined me to the step I had taken, she
made an exclamation of horror.

I told her that my intention was to remain

concealed till the search after me was over,
and then to embark for the continent.

She approved the project, and said, that
I could be no where in greater security than
with her; for, though the village is only six
miles from town, it is as much secluded as if
it was in the midst of a desert, except at the
feast of the holy Virgin which is celebrated
once a year.

The festival lasts nine days, and all the inhabitants of St. Jago come to assist at its cele-
bration. Unfortunately the season of the feast
was approashing, during which it would have
been impossible for me to remain concealed in
the village. However, as there was still time
to consider, she bade me be tranquil, and promised to find me a retreat. Two days after
she went to town and at her return I learned
that nothing was talked of but my elopement.

'St. Louis, in the first transports of his rage,
has entered a complaint against Don Alonzo
and, declaring that he had carried me off, had
him imprisoned !

It was feared this step would be attended
with ill consequences, for this young Spaniard,

s

being related to the bishop and some of the
most distinguished families, it was supposed
the indignity of his imprisonment would be
resented by them all!

Besides, he was entirely innocent of the
charge exhibited against him, not having had
the slightest idea of my flight

This information filled me with alarm.   I
felt insecure so near the town and entreated
madame V—— to indicate a more remote and
safe asylum.

She told me that she had a friend, twenty
leagues from town, to whom she had often
promised a visit; that the inconvenience of tra-
velling in this barbarous country, had hitherto
prevented her going, but that these considerations vanished before the idea of obliging me,
and that the pleasure of making the journey
in my company would be a sufficient induce-
ment.

Two days were past in procuring horses
and making preparations for our departure.
In the evening we walked among the rocks,
which surround the village, aud, had my heart

been at ease, I should have wandered with delight in these romantic regions.

The place was once famous for its valuable copper mines, from which it takes its name, but they have been long abandoned. The inhabitants, almost all mulattos, are in the last grade of poverty, and too indolent to make an exertion to procure themselves even the most necessary comforts. Yet, in this abode of wretchedness, there is a magnificent temple, dedicated to the blessed Virgin. Its ornaments and decorations are superb. The image of the Virgin, preserved in the temple, is said to be miraculous and performs often wonderful things. The faith of these people in her power is implicit. The site of the temple is picturesque, and the scenery, that surrounds it, beautiful beyond description, standing near the summit of a mountain, at the foot of which lies the village. You ascend to it by a winding road, and see its white turrets, at a great distance, glittering beneath the palm trees that gracefully wave over it.

After passing through the miserable village and following the winding path through crag-

gy cliffs, over barren rocks aud precipices
which the eye dares not measure, the mind
almost involuntarily yields to the belief of su-
pernatural agency. On entering the church
the image of the Virgin, fancifully adorned
and reposing on a bed of roses, appears like
the presiding genius of the place. The waxen
tapers, continually burning, the obscurity that
reigns within, occasioned by the impenetrable
branches of the trees which overshadow it, and
the slow solemn tone of the organ, re-echoed
by the surrounding rocks, fill the mind with
awe; and we pardon the superstitious faith of
the ignorant votaries of this holy lady, cherished as it is by every circumstance that can tend
to make it indelible !

At the appointed time, before the dawn of
day, our little cavalcade set out. Madame
V—— and myself on horseback, preceded by
a guide, and followed by a boy, leading two
mules charged with provisions, and every
thing requisite for the journey. We wore
large straw hats, to defend us from the sun,
with thick veils, according to the custom of
the country. Leaving Cobre behind us, we

ascended the mountain. The road passed through groves of majestic trees, intermingled with the orange and the lime, which being in blossom, the senses were almost overpowered by the odours which filled the air. We proceeded slowly and silently.—I thought of you my dear sister!—My tears flowed at the idea of your pain, and I trembled to think that I was not out of danger of being discovered.

About eight o'clock our guide said it was time to breakfast, and, tying our horses, he struck a light, kindled a fire, and made cho. colate. The repast finished, we continued on our way through the same delightful country; still breathing the purest air, but without discovering any vestige of a human habitation.

About noon we saw a little hut. The guide, alighting, half opened the door, saying "May the holy virgin bless this house!" This salutation brought out a tall sallow man, who gravely taking his segar from his mouth, bowed ceremoniously, and bid us enter. We followed him, and saw, sitting on an ox hide, stretched on the ground, a woman, whose ragged garments scarcely answered the first pur-

s 2

poses of decency. She was suckling a squalid
naked child, and two or three dirty children
were lolling about, without being disturbed
by the appearance of strangers. A hammock,
suspended from the roof, was the only article
of furniture in the house. Whilst the guide
was unloading the mules to prepare our dinner, I went out to seek a seat beneath some
trees; for the filth of the house, and the appearance of its inhabitants filled me with dis-
gust.

To my infinite astonishment, the plains
which extended behind the house, as far as
the eye could reach, were covered with innumerable herds of cattle, and on enquiring of
the guide to whom they belonged, I learned,
with no less surprise, that our host was their
master. Incredible as it may appear, this miserable looking being, whose abode resembled
the den of poverty, is the owner of countless
multitudes of cattle, and yet it was with the
greatest difficulty that we could procure a little milk.

A small piece of ground, where he raised
tobacco enough for his own use, was the only

vestige of cultivation we could discover. Nothing like vegetables or fruit could be seen.
When they kill a beef, they skin it, and, cut-
ting the flesh into long pieces about the thick-
ness of a finger, they hang it on poles to dry
in the sun ; and on this they live till it is gone,
and then kill another.

Sometimes they collect a number of cattle
and drive them to town, in order to procure
some of the most absolute necessaries of life.
But this seldom happens, and never till urged
by the most pressing want. As for bread, it
is a luxury with which they are entirely unacquainted. After dinner the guide, and the host,
and all the family, lay down on the ground to
sleep the siesta, which, you know no consideration would tempt a Spaniard to forget. Madame V—— walked with me under the trees,
near the house, and remarked the striking dif-
ference between this country and St. Domingo.
There, every inch of ground was in the highest
state of cultivation, and every body was rich,
here, the owners of vast territories are in the
most abject poverty.

This she ascribed to the different genius of

the people, but I think unjustly, believing that
it is entirely owing to their vicious government.

After our guide had taken his nap he led
up the horses, and bidding adieu to our hosts,
we continued our journey.

We passed during the afternoon several
habitations similar to the one where we dined.
The same wretchedness; the same poverty
exhibited itself, surrounded by troops of cattle, who bathed in plains of the most luxuriant
pasturage.

As the sun declined our guide began to
sing a litany to the Virgin, in which he was
joined by the boy who followed us. The
strain was sweet.

> " And round a holy calm diffusing
> In melancholy murmurs died away."

At the close of day we stopped at a hut,
where the guide told us we must pass the
night, and I learned that we had come ten
leagues, though we had advanced at a snail's
pace. The hut we entered was inhabited by
an old man who, retiring with the guide to an
adjoining shed, left us the house to ourselves.

The couch, which invited us to repose, was a hide laid on the ground. Madame V——— had brought sheets, and, spreading them on the hide, I soon sunk to rest. But my slumbers were interrupted by a most unaccountable noise, which seemed to issue from all parts of the room, not unlike the clashing of swords ; and, as I listened to discover what it was, a shriek from Madame V——— increased my terror. In sounds scarcely articulate, she said a large cold animal had crept into her bosom, and in getting it out, it had seized her hand.

Frightened to death I opened the door and called the guide, who discovered by his laughing that he had foreseen our misfortune, and guarded against it by suspending his hammock from the branches of a tree. When I asked for a light to search for what had disturbed us, he said it was nothing but land crabs, which, at this season, descend in countless multitudes from the mountain, in order to lay their eggs on the sea shore.

The ground was covered with them, and paths were worn by them down the sides of

the mountain. They strike their claws together as they move with a strange noise, and
no obstacle turns them from their course.
Had they not found a passage through the
house they would have gone over it; and one
finding madame V—— in his way, had crept
into her bosom. The master of the house
gave his hammock to madame V——. I
mounted in that of the guide; but the curiosity excited by our visitors, rendered it impossible for us to sleep. I asked the guide if
it was common to see them in such numbers.
He said that it was; and told me that the English having some years ago made a descent
on the island, had seized a Spaniard whom
they found in a hut, and threatened to kill him
if he would not shew them the way to St.
Jago, which they had always wished to possess, but which they could not approach by
sea. The terrified Spaniard promised to com-
ply. In the night, as they were encamped on
the mountain, waiting for daylight in order to
proceed, they heard a noise stealing through
the thickets, like that of an approaching host.
They asked their prisoner what it meant? he

replied, that it could be nothing but a body of Spaniards who, apprized of their descent, were preparing to attack them. The noise increasing on all sides, the English, fearful of being surrounded, embarked, and in their haste suffered the prisoner to escape, who by his address probably prevented them from becoming masters of the island, for the pretended host was nothing more than an army of these crabs.

The man, I understand, received no reward; but the anniversary of this event is still celebrated; and if the crabs have not been canonized, they are at least spoken of with as much reverence as the sacred geese, to which Rome owed its preservation.

During the night their noise prevented me effectually from sleeping. They appeared like a brown stream rolling over the surface of the earth. Towards morning they gradually disappeared, hiding themselves in holes during the day.

At the first peep of dawn we set out, and arrived in the evening at Bayam. The friend of madame V—— received us with great cordiality. She lost her husband soon after her

arrival in this country. She is very handsome,
and has an air of sadness which renders her
highly interesting. She was informed of my
story, and requested me to think myself at
home in her house.

It was determined that I should pass for a
relation of her husband; and soothed by her
kindness and attentions I began to hope that
beneath her roof I should find repose.

Madame V——, after staying with us
eight days, returned to Cobre, promising to
inform herself of you, and to write me all that
was passing. She wrote me immediately that
you had sailed for Jamaica: that Don Alonzo
was out of prison; that he had commenced a
suit against St. Louis for false imprisonment,
and that the latter was actually confined. Don
Alonzo is powerfully supported by the bishop
and all his family, who have long been at variance with the governor, and gladly seek this
opportunity of revenging themselves. She
finally told me, my dear Mary, that she had
discovered a young man who owned a small
vessel in which he goes constantly to Jamaica,
and that she had entreated him to find you, to

ST. DOMINGO.   205

tell you that I am well, and to charge himself
with your letter, not doubting but you would
write. That kind letter I received yesterday,
and it has given me the first agreeable sensa-
tion I have known since we parted. I am
convinced of your affection for me, but do not
let that affection hurry you into imprudencies
which may perhaps betray me. Do not think
of returning to St. Jago; and, may I add, do
not think of leaving Jamaica till I can join you.
We will return to the continent together, and
I hope together we shall he happy. Two or
three doubloons, which I brought with me,
prevent my being dependant on the lady in
whose house I am, for any thing but her friendship.

I was struck with the resemblance of a
Spanish lady who lives near us to Don Alonzo, and found, on enquiring, that she is his
sister. She spoke to me of her brother, but is
as ignorant of his affairs as if he dwelt in the
moon.

This place is the abode of poverty and dull-
ness, yet the people are so hospitable that from

T

the little they possess they can always spare something to offer to a stranger. And they are content with their lot—how many reasons have I not to be so with mine !

LETTER XXIX.

—

To Mary ——

Bayam.

I thank you a thousand times, my dear sister, for your affectionate letter, and for the parcel that accompanied it. I knew with what pleasure you would share with me all you possess, and to be indebted to you adds to my happiness.

What you have heard of St. Louis is true. The affair of Don Alonzo and himself was made up by the interposition of some of their mutual friends who represented him as half mad; and somebody having spread a report that I had sailed for the city of Santo Domingo, he embarked immediately for that place. What he could think I should seek at Santo Domingo, I am at a loss to imagine.

My retreat has been discovered, and though
by one who would not betray me, yet he is the
last person on earth, except St. Louis, to whom
I could have wished it to be known.

The husband of Donna Maria, the Spanish
lady whom I mentioned to you before, had
gone to St. Jago, some days previous to my
arrival here. Having, as is the universal custom, visited a gaming house, he had a dispute
with a gambler of bad reputation, and on leaving the house received a blow with a poinard,
which proved mortal.

Such occurrences are too frequent to create
much public interest, and it is considered use-
less to seek the assassin.

When the senora Maria expected the return of her husband, she heard that he existed
no longer. The news was brought by her brother. Her house joins the one I live in. Hearing the most lamentable cries from her chamber I ran in. Judge of my surprise at seeing
Don Alonzo. His, I believe, was not less, for
abandoning his sister, he approached me; but
I was too much terrified at her situation, to
attend to him. When informed of the cause,

I felt that in that moment she could not be consoled, and I saw also that the violence of her sorrow would soon exhaust itself.

Don Alonzo sought an opportunity of speaking to me, which I avoided. Learning afterwards where I lived, he so ingratiated himself with madame St. Clair, that he received an invitation to her house, and in that house he now passes all his time. He has been the innocent cause of much of my suffering, yet I cannot find fault with his conduct; and madame St. Clair, devoting much of her time to his widowed sister, I have no means of escaping from him. He has informed me of many of the follies of St. Louis, of the obstinacy with which he affirmed that Don Alonzo had aided my flight, and of the means he had employed to discover me. And why, he sometimes asks, did you not suffer me to aid you? why did you not repose confidence in me?

You know my dear Mary, how eloquent are his eyes! you know the insinuating softness of his voice! Sometimes, when listening to him, I forget for a moment all I have suf-

T 2

fered, and almost persuade myself that a man can be sincere.

The governor of Bayam is an Irish Spaniard, at least he is of an Irish family, and was born in Spain. I have become acquainted with him since the arrival of Don Alonzo, and felt, the instant I beheld him, as if I was in the society of an old acquaintance. His Irish vivacity is a little tempered by Spanish gravity. He speaks English as if he had been raised in his own country, and his mind is stored with literary treasures. He has a handsome collection of books, which he offered me. Judge of my delight at meeting with Shakspeare in the wilds of Cuba.

What could have induced him to accept this sorry government I have not yet learned, but he certainly possesses talents which merit a more important employment, and his elegant manners would add lustre to the most distinguished situation. He laughs heartily at his ragged subjects, by whom however he is regarded as a father and a friend. He says with better laws they would be the best fellows in the world; but situated as they are, their indolence is their best security.

We often make excursions in the beatiful environs of this place and dine beneath the shade of the palm tree, or the tall and graceful cocoa, which offers us in its fruit a delicious dessert, whilst the gaiety of the governor diffuses around us an indescribable charm.

But my dear sister, think not that I forget you in these delightful scenes. On the contrary I long to see you, and am hastening the moment of my departure.

Madame St. Clair, seduced by the description I have made of our peaceful country, and wearied of a place where she has known nothing but misfortune, where the talents she possesses are absolutely lost, intends going with me to Philadelphia, as soon as she can arrange her affairs, and has consented to accompany me to Kingston, from whence we can all sail together. You will love her, I am sure, for her kindness to me; but, independently of that consideration, her beauty, the graceful sweetness of her manners, and her divine voice, render it impossible to behold or listen to her with indifference.

The governor says, if he loses his two most amiable subjects, his little empire will not be worth keeping.   Don Alonzo

"Looks and sighs unutterable things,"

and sometimes hints, in broken accents, the passion he has felt for me since the first moment he saw me, at all which I laugh.   For me, henceforth all men are statues.   I was so ill-fated as to meet that phenomenon a jealous Frenchman, and with my wounds still bleeding, would I put my happiness in the power of a Spaniard? Ah! no, let me avoid the dangerous intercourse, let me fly to my sister! Why are you so far removed from me? why did you so hastily leave the island, where you knew I must be, and in a situation too in which your counsel, your support is doubly necessary.

It will be impossible for me to leave Bayam in less than a month.   We shall sail for Kingston with Anselmo.   Much precaution must be used, for I must embark from St.

Jago, and if I was discovered, should certainly be arrested by the governor, who is exasperated against me. Write to me, my dear
girl, by the return of the vessel; and believe
me that I wait with the utmost impatience for
the moment that will reunite us.

215

LETTER XXX.

—

To Clara.

Kingston.

Let me entreat you, my dear sister, to
leave Bayam as soon as possible. I cannot
describe the pain with which I heard of Don
Alonzo being near you. You pass hours,
days with him; you talk of his eloquent eyes,
his sweet voice. Ah! fly, dearest creature,
fly from the danger that surrounds you. Listen not to that insinuating Spaniard. If you do
you are irrecoverably lost.

Why indeed am I not near you? yet after
your flight, to stay in Cuba was impossible,
and my leaving it was, I believe, one of the
principal reasons which determined St. Louis
to leave it also: so far it was fortunate. My
heart always acquitted you for having taken

the resolution to abandon your home ; for
though, as you say, I knew not all, I knew
enough to awaken in my breast every sensa-
tion of pity. Yet it is not sufficient that you
are acquitted by a sister, who will always be
thought partial; and if you cannot conciliate general approbation, at least endeavour to avoid
meriting general censure. Who that hears of
your being at Bayam, in the house of the sister of Don Alonzo, knowing that he had been
publicly accused of having taken you off, and
learns, that as soon as the affair was hushed up
in St. Jago, that he went to Bayam, that he
passes all his time in your society, that at
home and abroad he is ever at your side, who
can hear all this, and not believe that it was
preconcerted? Ah! Clara, Clara, I believe
that it was not, because I love you, and cannot think you would deceive me. But why
stay a month, a week, a day, where you are?
Why not come to me when Anselmo returns?
when with me, my friendship, my affection,
will soothe and console you. I will remove
from your lacerated breast the thorns which
have been planted there by the hand of misfor-

tune. You shall forget your sorrows, and I
will aid you against your own heart, for I believe at present *that* is your most dangerous
enemy.

219

LETTER XXXI.

To MARY ——

Bayam.

You frighten me to death, my dear sister, with your apprehensions. You paint my situation in terrifying colours; yet could I forsee that I should be led into it, when alone and friendless I fled at midnight from a house where I suffered continual torture? Did I imagine that in Bayam I should become acquainted with Don Alonzo's sister, and that I should meet him in her house? Sentence, I know, has been passed against me, and that sentence will be confirmed by what has happened subsequent to my elopement. The testimony of my own heart will be of little avail. But will you also join against me? I cannot believe it. Condemn me not, at least suspend all opinion till we meet, which will be in a fortnight. To avoid the danger of passing through St. Jago, we go by land to a place called Portici, from whence we shall embark. The journey will be delightful. We intend making it on horseback. The governor and Don Alonzo will accompany us. Start not at this, for it cannot be otherwise; nor could I, by refusing his services, discover that I thought it dangerous to accept them.

In my anxiety to see you, every moment seems an age, yet I feel something like regret at leaving this country. The friendliness of the people can never be forgotten. Here, as in Barracoa, they are poor but contented. They sip their chocolate, smoke a segar, and thrum the guitar undisturbed by care. Often, when reviewing the events of my past life, I wish that their calm destiny had been mine; but alas! how different has been my fate.

I write this letter to prepare you for my arrival. When Anselmo goes next, I go with him; and, when I embrace my sister, I shall be happy.

LETTER XXXII.

———

Kingston, Jamaica.

Clara, my dear friend, is at length arrived. I have held that truant girl to my heart, and have forgotten whilst embracing her all the reproaches I intended to make, and which I thought she deserved. I cannot help loving her, though I approve not of all she does; but I will blame her fate rather than herself, for who can behold her and not believe that she is all goodness? who can witness the powers of her mind and withhold their admiration? Whatever subject may engage her attention, she seizes intuitively on what is true, and by a sort of mental magic, arrives instantaneous-ly at the point where, even very good heads, only meet her after a tedious process of reasoning and reflection. Her memory, surer than records, perpetuates every occurrence.

She accumulates knowledge while she laughs and plays: she steals from her friends the fruits of their application, and thus becoming possessed of their intellectual treasure, without the fatigue of study, she surprises them with ingenious combinations of their own materials, and with results of which they did not dream. Her heart keeps a faithful account, not only of every word but of every look, of every movement of her friends, prompted by kindness and affection, and never is her society more delightful than in those moments of calm and sublime meditation, when her genius surveys the past, or wanders through a fanciful and novel arrangement of the future. Who that thus knows Clara, and is sensible of her worth, can have known her husband, and condemn her?

It is true, Clara is said to be a coquette, but have not ladies of superior talents and attractions, at all times and in all countries been subject to that censure? unless indeed theirs was the rare fortune of becoming early in life attached to a man equal or superior to themselves! Attachments between such people last through

life, and are always new. Love continues because love has existed; interests create interests; parental are added to conjugal affections; with the multiplicity of domestic objects the number of domestic joys increase.
In such a situation the heart is always occupied, and always full. For those who live in
it their home is the world; their feelings, their
powers, their talents are employed. They go
into society as they take a ramble; it affords
transient amusement, but becomes not a habit.
Their thoughts, their wishes dwell at home,
and they are good because they are happy.
But if on the contrary a woman is disappointed in the first object of her affections, or if separated from him she loved, fate connects her
with an inferior being, to what can it lead?
You might as well expect to confine a sprightly boy, in all the vigour of health to sedate in-
action, as to prevent talents and beauty, thus
circumstanced, from courting admiration. A
feeling heart seeks for corresponding emo-
tions; and when a woman, like Clara, can fas-
cinate, intoxicate, transport, and whilst unhappy is surrounded by seductive objects, she

will become entangled, and be borne away by the rapidity of her own sensations, happy if she can stop short on the brink of destruction.

If Clara's husband had been in every respect worthy of her she would have been one of the best and happiest of human beings, but her good qualities were lost on him; and, though he might have made a very good husband to a woman of ordinary capacity, to Clara he became a tyrant.

Sensible of the impossibility of her leaving him, he took it for granted that she bestowed on another those sentiments he could not hope to awaken himself. Yet Clara never deceived him. There is in her character a proud frankness which renders her averse to, and unfit for intrigue. When at the Cape, she was not dazzled by splendor, though it courted her acceptance; nor could the ill-treatment of her husband force her to seek a refuge from it in the arms of a lover who had the means of protecting her. At St. Jago his conduct became more insupportable, and when at length she fled from his house, alone and friendless, she was unseduced by love, but impelled by a repugnance for her husband which had reached its height, and could no longer be resisted.

Delivered from the weight of this oppressive sentiment, she now enjoys a delightful tranquillity, which even the thought of many approaching struggles with difficulty and distress, cannot disturb.

In such a situation I am more than ever necessary to my sister; and, perhaps, it is the consciousness of this, that has given birth to many of the sentiments expressed in this letter.

We have learned that St. Louis sailed from the city of Santo Domingo to France, from which I hope he may never return.

Clara and myself will leave this for Philadelphia, in the course of the ensuing week. There I hope we shall meet you; and if I can only infuse into your bosom those sentiments for my sister which glow so warmly in my own, she will find in you a friend and a protector, and we may still be happy.

THE END.

For EU product safety concerns, contact us at Calle de José Abascal, 56–1°, 28003 Madrid, Spain or eugpsr@cambridge.org.

www.ingramcontent.com/pod-product-compliance
Ingram Content Group UK Ltd.
Pitfield, Milton Keynes, MK11 3LW, UK
UKHW010337140625
459647UK00010B/649